HowExpert Guide to Ephemera Collectibles

101+ Tips to ~~~ v to Buy, Sell, Au ~~~ Care for Your ~~~ ection

HowExpert with Charlotte Hopkins

Copyright HowExpert™
www.HowExpert.com

For more tips related to this topic, visit
HowExpert.com/ephemeracollectibles.

Recommended Resources

- HowExpert.com – How To Guides on All Topics from A to Z by Everyday Experts.
- HowExpert.com/free – Free HowExpert Email Newsletter.
- HowExpert.com/books – HowExpert Books
- HowExpert.com/courses – HowExpert Courses
- HowExpert.com/clothing – HowExpert Clothing
- HowExpert.com/membership – HowExpert Membership Site
- HowExpert.com/affiliates – HowExpert Affiliate Program
- HowExpert.com/jobs – HowExpert Jobs
- HowExpert.com/writers – Write About Your #1 Passion/Knowledge/Expertise & Become a HowExpert Author.
- HowExpert.com/resources – Additional HowExpert Recommended Resources
- YouTube.com/HowExpert – Subscribe to HowExpert YouTube.
- Instagram.com/HowExpert – Follow HowExpert on Instagram.
- Facebook.com/HowExpert – Follow HowExpert on Facebook.
- TikTok.com/@HowExpert – Follow HowExpert on TikTok.

Publisher's Foreword

Dear HowExpert Reader,

HowExpert publishes quick 'how to' guides on all topics from A to Z by everyday experts.

At HowExpert, our mission is to discover, empower, and maximize everyday people's talents to ultimately make a positive impact in the world for all topics from A to Z...one everyday expert at a time!

All of our HowExpert guides are written by everyday people just like you and me, who have a passion, knowledge, and expertise for a specific topic.

We take great pride in selecting everyday experts who have a passion, real-life experience in a topic, and excellent writing skills to teach you about the topic you are also passionate about and eager to learn.

We hope you get a lot of value from our HowExpert guides, and it can make a positive impact on your life in some way. All of our readers, including you, help us continue living our mission of positively impacting the world for all spheres of influences from A to Z.

If you enjoyed one of our HowExpert guides, then please take a moment to send us your feedback from wherever you got this book.

Thank you, and we wish you all the best in all aspects of life.

Sincerely,

BJ Min
Founder & Publisher of HowExpert
HowExpert.com

PS...If you are also interested in becoming a HowExpert author, then please visit our website at HowExpert.com/writers. Thank you & again, all the best!

COPYRIGHT, LEGAL NOTICE AND DISCLAIMER:

COPYRIGHT © BY HOWEXPERT™ (OWNED BY HOT METHODS, INC.). ALL RIGHTS RESERVED WORLDWIDE. NO PART OF THIS PUBLICATION MAY BE REPRODUCED IN ANY FORM OR BY ANY MEANS, INCLUDING SCANNING, PHOTOCOPYING, OR OTHERWISE WITHOUT PRIOR WRITTEN PERMISSION OF THE COPYRIGHT HOLDER.

DISCLAIMER AND TERMS OF USE: PLEASE NOTE THAT MUCH OF THIS PUBLICATION IS BASED ON PERSONAL EXPERIENCE AND ANECDOTAL EVIDENCE. ALTHOUGH THE AUTHOR AND PUBLISHER HAVE MADE EVERY REASONABLE ATTEMPT TO ACHIEVE COMPLETE ACCURACY OF THE CONTENT IN THIS GUIDE, THEY ASSUME NO RESPONSIBILITY FOR ERRORS OR OMISSIONS. ALSO, YOU SHOULD USE THIS INFORMATION AS YOU SEE FIT, AND AT YOUR OWN RISK. YOUR PARTICULAR SITUATION MAY NOT BE EXACTLY SUITED TO THE EXAMPLES ILLUSTRATED HERE; IN FACT, IT'S LIKELY THAT THEY WON'T BE THE SAME, AND YOU SHOULD ADJUST YOUR USE OF THE INFORMATION AND RECOMMENDATIONS ACCORDINGLY.

THE AUTHOR AND PUBLISHER DO NOT WARRANT THE PERFORMANCE, EFFECTIVENESS OR APPLICABILITY OF ANY SITES LISTED OR LINKED TO IN THIS BOOK. ALL LINKS ARE FOR INFORMATION PURPOSES ONLY AND ARE NOT WARRANTED FOR CONTENT, ACCURACY OR ANY OTHER IMPLIED OR EXPLICIT PURPOSE.

ANY TRADEMARKS, SERVICE MARKS, PRODUCT NAMES OR NAMED FEATURES ARE ASSUMED TO BE THE PROPERTY OF THEIR RESPECTIVE OWNERS, AND ARE USED ONLY FOR REFERENCE. THERE IS NO IMPLIED ENDORSEMENT IF WE USE ONE OF THESE TERMS.

NO PART OF THIS BOOK MAY BE REPRODUCED, STORED IN A RETRIEVAL SYSTEM, OR TRANSMITTED BY ANY OTHER MEANS: ELECTRONIC, MECHANICAL, PHOTOCOPYING, RECORDING, OR OTHERWISE, WITHOUT THE PRIOR WRITTEN PERMISSION OF THE AUTHOR.

ANY VIOLATION BY STEALING THIS BOOK OR DOWNLOADING OR SHARING IT ILLEGALLY WILL BE PROSECUTED BY LAWYERS TO THE FULLEST EXTENT. THIS PUBLICATION IS PROTECTED UNDER THE US COPYRIGHT ACT OF 1976 AND ALL OTHER APPLICABLE INTERNATIONAL, FEDERAL, STATE AND LOCAL LAWS AND ALL RIGHTS ARE RESERVED, INCLUDING RESALE RIGHTS: YOU ARE NOT ALLOWED TO GIVE OR SELL THIS GUIDE TO ANYONE ELSE.

THIS PUBLICATION IS DESIGNED TO PROVIDE ACCURATE AND AUTHORITATIVE INFORMATION WITH REGARD TO THE SUBJECT MATTER COVERED. IT IS SOLD WITH THE UNDERSTANDING THAT THE AUTHORS AND PUBLISHERS ARE NOT ENGAGED IN RENDERING LEGAL, FINANCIAL, OR OTHER PROFESSIONAL ADVICE. LAWS AND PRACTICES OFTEN VARY FROM STATE TO STATE AND IF LEGAL OR OTHER EXPERT ASSISTANCE IS REQUIRED, THE SERVICES OF A PROFESSIONAL SHOULD BE SOUGHT. THE AUTHORS AND PUBLISHER SPECIFICALLY DISCLAIM ANY LIABILITY THAT IS INCURRED FROM THE USE OR APPLICATION OF THE CONTENTS OF THIS BOOK.

COPYRIGHT BY HOWEXPERT™ (OWNED BY HOT METHODS, INC.)
ALL RIGHTS RESERVED WORLDWIDE.

Table of Contents

Recommended Resources 2
Publisher's Foreword 3
Chapter 1: Jump Start Your Ephemera Collection 6
   Starting an Ephemera Collection 6
Chapter 2: Ephemera Categories ~ Entertaining and Historical 17
   Understanding Ephemera Categories Part One 17
Chapter 3: Ephemera Categories ~ Everyday Ephemera 31
   Understanding Ephemera Categories Part Two 31
Chapter 4: Ephemera History 44
   A History in Ephemera 44
Chapter 5: The Ephemera Community 66
   The Importance of Meeting Collectors 66
Chapter 6: Collectors Celebrating Ephemera 76
   Celebrating and Recognizing Collectibles 76
Chapter 7: Care Rules for Ephemera Collectors .. 87
   Protecting, Preserving, and Displaying Your Ephemera 87
Chapter 8: Buying, Selling, and Authenticating Ephemera 101
   Maneuvering the Process of Buying and Selling Ephemera 101
About the Expert 117
About the Publisher 118
Recommended Resources 119

Chapter 1: Jump Start Your Ephemera Collection

- Getting Started Collecting Ephemera
- Keep Excellent Records
- Filling a Junk Journal
- Recognize the Signs of Aging
- Know the Ephemera Lingo

Starting an Ephemera Collection

Ephemera are items made from paper that were not made to last. Fortunately, collectors swooped in and rescued many pieces of ephemera from being tossed away. These paper treasures, when pieced together, form a timeline of history. They include ticket stubs, candy wrappers, advertisements, chapbooks, postcards, stickers, stamps, labels, watch papers, magazines, and even air sickness bags. Collecting ephemera has been growing in popularity, and with each piece carrying a favorite memory, the popularity of ephemera will only continue to grow.

Tip 1: Starting an Ephemera Collection

The best part about collecting ephemera is that you can start a collection at any time with a minimal investment since this is an inexpensive hobby that is low maintenance. Where to start depends on which of those collectible paper pieces draws you near. Ephemera themes can include movies & plays, holidays, business, games, and old school. If you enjoy traveling, consider booklets, travel logs, and maps. If you have a favorite animal, such as penguins or elephants, you can collect animal ephemera that features your favorite. Animal ephemera can be found on posters, brochures, booklets, greeting cards, postcards, and decorations. Some ephemera collectors have a favorite region or time period. Paper collectibles can be found all over, so to get started choosing your favorite ephemera pieces or just go all in and collect a wide variety. The choice is all yours.

Tip 2: Consider These First

Looking for ideas? Here are some suggestions to get started. Lost pet posters, embroidery cards, color charts, ink charts, laundry lists, seating plans, and attendance records for schools, churches, organizations, and even funerals have attendance cards. Church-related ephemera are programs, mass cards, hymn sheets, communion cards, altar cards, Bible cards, and confirmation cards. Mind maps are diagrams that outline ideas and information; they center around a single word with more concepts added on to that.

There is also a selection of medical ephemera to choose from, such as eye charts, vaccination records, medical records, apothecary labels, medicine labels, accident report forms, CPR and rescue charts, appointment cards, and medical certificates.

Lists make great additions to ephemera collections. Popular lists are reading lists, wine lists, casualty lists, checklists, donation lists, gift lists, price lists, soldier wish lists, commissary lists, inventories, and staff lists.

Holiday ephemera makes a fun and colorful section of paper! Types of holiday ephemera are party hats, paper glasses, Round Robin Letters (Christmas letters), Christmas cards, Valentines, masks, catalogs, paper garland, gift tags, stickers, and wrapping paper.

Tip 3: What Kind of Ephemera Collector Will You Be?

Stamps are the most popular item collected today, and those collectors are known as Philatelists. These are names derived through the years that describe specific types of ephemera collectors:

- Aerophilately – The hobby of collecting airmail.
- Brandophilists – A person who collects cigar bands.
- Cartophilist – A person who collects cigarette cards and trading cards.
- Deltiologist – A person who collects, studies, and preserves postcards.
- Labologist – A person who collects beer bottle labels.
- Lexicographer – A person who collects dictionaries.
- Lotologist – A person who collects lottery tickets.
- Notaphilist – A person who collects paper money.
- Pannapictagraphist – A person who collects comic books.
- Phillumenist – A person who collects matchbooks and matchboxes.
- Sucrology – The hobby of collecting sugar packets

Tip 4: Places to Find Ephemera Pieces

Paper products are all around us, so there are many places to find ephemera pieces for your collection. Flea markets, used bookstores, estate sales, and thrift shops are popular places to start. Family ephemera includes birth certificates, deeds, mortgages, receipts, and letters. Ephemera can sometimes be bought in bulk from swap meets and online auction sites. Library book sales and antique malls are a few more prime sources for finding vintage ephemera.

Do not forget about your own environment. Check inside your home, around your church, and even inside your own glove box. You may find eye-catching images online that will look great in your collection. You can capture scenes from vintage books on the "Old Book Illustrations" website (oldbookillustrations.com). The website for the Library of Congress (https://www.loc.gov/free-to-use/) and the Smithsonian Library (https://library.si.edu/books-online) offer images on hundreds of topics that you can add to your ephemera collection. On Etsy, sellers offer vintage photographs and ephemera in bundles, including junk journal kits.

Tip 5: The Different Types of Paper

Papyrus is a type of paper first used in Egypt in 2900 BC. Today papyrus is used by artists and for writing calligraphy. Lokta paper is soft, and Laid paper has a ribbed texture. In the 1700s, the majority of paper was crafted from cotton and linen rags. In the 1800s, most papers were made from wood pulp, manila, and straw. Rag paper is a high-quality style of paper that is used for banknotes, certificates, legal documents, vellum, and tracing paper. Other types of paper to consider adding when collecting ephemera are wrapping paper, blotting paper, carbon paper, recycled paper, tissue paper, newspaper print, hemp paper, paperboard, and cardstock.

Tip 6: Signs of Aging on Paper

The minute that paper is manufactured, it begins to break down. The most common sign of aging to paper is yellowing. Foxing, creasing, tears, dirt, and water damage also occur over time.

Lignin is used to make paper; in time, the acid from lignin starts to leak and causes the paper to discolor and crumble.

There is a difference between a crease and a wrinkle. Creases go all the way through the paper and leave a discolored or white line; wrinkles are more of a wavy defect on the paper. Collectors should not attempt to fix these. Leave that up to the professionals. They have the equipment to straighten wrinkles; some can fix the discolored or white lines left by a crease.

Tip 7: Error Card Mistakes Sought after by Collectors

Both sports enthusiasts and ephemera collectors collect baseball cards and trading cards. Through the years, a number of cards were released with errors, including the wrong dates or names and sometimes the wrong photo. These are called "error cards." These are just some of the error cards produced.

In 1910, Sherry Magee had his last name misspelled on his baseball card. Instead, it was spelled as "Magie." The mistake helped make this one of Topps's most valuable baseball cards ever made. Even in poor condition, the value does not change.

In 1952, Topps released the Johnny Sain baseball card with Joe Paige's biography information on the back. And Joe Paige's baseball card had Sain's information on the back. Another aspect of Sain's baseball card that makes it valuable is its black coloring on the back. This is rare among baseball cards.

The 1969 Topps Mickey Mantle baseball card has two versions. One has his name in white letters, and the other has his name in yellow letters. The card with the white letters is considered the error card and has continued to increase in value.

In 1989, when Bill Ripken posed for his Fleer baseball card, he did not realize that the words "Fuck Face" were written on the bottom of the bat.

The Topps Frank Thomas Rookie Card from 1990 is completely missing his name on the front.

The website Baseball Errors (www.baseballerrors.com) has a list of every error card manufactured. Though most error cards are connected to baseball, it did not only happen with that sport. One example is the 1954 Bowman Emlen Tunnell card. They misspelled his last name. They left off the letter "l" and spelled it "Tunnel."

Tip 8: Steps to Fill in a Junk Journal

A junk journal is a handmade book that is used to fill with ephemera pieces. People include bookmarks, greeting cards, postcards, photographs, paper dolls, tickets, business cards, and trade stamps in their junk journals. What you put on the pages of your junk journal should be the cherished paper pieces that are most important to you. The key difference between a junk journal and a scrapbook is the size. A scrapbook has large thick pages. A junk journal is typically handmade and the size of a notebook. A notebook can even be used as a junk journal. Covers for junk journals can be made from old book covers and cereal boxes.

Tip 9: Defining Different Types of Labels

Collecting fruit labels is a large part of the ephemera community. It is in a category of its own. These are the different types of labels used on fruit:

Bag Labels – These labels are found on the bag itself and not directly on the fruit.

Box Labels – The labels found on boxes and crates that growers used to ship fruit to the grocery store.

Documentation Labels – These labels usually show an image of the fruit. They can also be detached easily and reapplied somewhere else.

Hang Tags – these are labels that are tied to the fruit. This is usually done because these labels contain more information and images.

Promotion Tags – These tags are attached to fruit passed out during events or included in a wholesale order.

Tip 10: The Ephemera Grading Scale

When determining the value of ephemera, collectors use a scale with 14 different categories.

Mint (MT) – The paper is flat with only light fading. The corners have no folds or tears. There cannot be any rust lines from the presence of staples.

Mint/Near Mint (M/NM) – This is similar to Mint. This piece would have only slight blemishes.

Near Mint (NM) – The color shows minimal fading. There may be staple marks but no rust.qq**Near Mint/Very Fine (NM/VF)** – There are some negative qualities that keep it from being "near mint," but it is slightly better than "very fine."

Very Fine (VF) – The item does not have to be perfectly flat. There can be some discoloring around the staples. Also, the item can have small tears and a yellow hue around the edge.

Very Fine/Fine (VF/F) – The quality is slightly better than fine.

Fine (F) – The item has minor surface wear and may show light stress marks. It can have a tear that is less than half an inch, as long as it does not include the color or letters and no large creases.

Fine/Very Good (F/VG) – The item is slightly better than Very Good.

Very Good (VG) – Can have a center crease or shaped from being rolled. It can have discoloring, fading, and a corner tear no larger than a quarter inch. The edge can have folds, creases, and minor tears. There can be some rusting around the staples. The border can show browning but no crumbling.

Very Good/Good (VG/G) – The quality is slightly better than Good.

Good (G) – Can have missing pieces no larger than half an inch. It can have a tear, no larger than two inches but no signs of crumbling. The image can show fading, and it can have creases and scuff marks.

Good/Fair (G/FR) – Slightly better than fair condition.

Fair (FR) – The item is soiled and scuffed, showing folds, creases, and stains. It may have missing pieces and tears that are 2/3 the length of the paper.

Poor (PR) – The item has large stains, missing staples, brittle, and crumbling. The item has missing pieces, mildew, and heavy scuff marks. It can have markings, glue, and tape marks.

Tip 11: Working with Ephemera Dealers

When you work with antique dealers, keep in mind that the price is negotiable. Sometimes dealers will take trades.

The Ephemera Society website has a list of ephemera dealers that can help you on your journey with buying and selling ephemera (www.ephemerasociety.org/dealer-member-websites).

Most antiques and collectibles dealers can be trusted, but not all of them. Research information and quotes that they give you upon meeting them. You will learn which ones you can trust. When you do find antique dealers that you trust, you can give them a list of items you would like for your collection. Then, they have resources to help find them.

Tip 12: Ephemera Lingo for Collectors

Ephemera is defined as "something of no lasting significance" and "collectibles not intended to have lasting value." Paper items (such as posters, broadsides, and tickets) that were originally meant to be discarded after use but have since become collectibles. As an ephemera collector, these terms are also important to remember. Some collectors choose to make their own album pages with cardstock. When doing this, make sure the cardstock is acid and lignin free.

Acid-free – Paper that has a neutral PH balance.

Advertising Covers (ad covers) – Envelopes that include illustrations and images on the front.

Age Toning – The yellow and brown color that develops on paper through aging.

Archives – A collection of vintage and historical documents.

Art Print – A reproduction of an original piece of artwork.

Bleed – When the printing on top of the paper extends over the edge of the trim.

Bobtail - A matchbook that has the striker cut off.

Brother Jonathan – A fictional character that depicted the everyday American. He was the predecessor to Uncle Sam.

Centering – When the white border around trading cards is the same size on all four sides.

Cockling – When wrinkles are formed in the paper during the drying process caused by high amounts of ink, causing the paper fibers to swell. This is sometimes called waviness.

Corner Indents – When slight dips and impressions develop near the four corners.

Crazing – This happens when photographs and cards with a glossy image develop a fine line of cracks similar to a spider web look.

Crease/Wrinkle – A photograph or paper product is produced in layers. When there is a bend that shows on both sides, that is called a crease. When the bend is only showing on one side, it is called a wrinkle.

Cross Collectible – An item that is sought after by different types of collectors.

Dimensional Stability – A measure of how much paper will shrink in size during printing.

Incunabula – A book that was printed before 1501.

Flats - Matchbook covers that never held matches and were carried by salesmen.

Foxing – Small yellow and brown blotches on paper caused by mold and iron deposits in the paper.

Fuzzy Edges – A texture along the edge of trading cards that feels fuzzy. This happens when it is not cut straight during production.

Laid Paper – A type of paper manufactured with a ribbed texture.

Print Defect – This is also called a "print line" or a "print dot." This is when a line, a dot, or a series of dots appears inside the image. An error causes this in the printing process.

Trimmed – A paper item that has been cut to a different size.

Tip 13: Keep Detailed Records

Keeping good records is important for any collector. This will help you to remember what you have so you do not buy more than one. The notes you keep will also be beneficial if you choose to sell any parts of your ephemera collection. When you add ephemera to your collection, take note of when and where you received it and how much it cost. Also, write down any information that you have on the history of the item, whether it was a wrapper from a trip to a unique candy store or a postcard from a young writer that lived in the 1800s.

Describe the condition of the paper pieces. Note any wrinkles, spots, or tears. Look up the current value of the item and note that, also. If you purchased the item from someone, note how much you paid and the seller's full name and contact information. Try to get their full address. You will need this in case you need to reach the buyer again. If the ephemera was ever stored, note when and where it was saved. Also, write the details of how it was saved. If you take precautionary measures, note specifically what they were.

Chapter 2: Ephemera Categories ~ Entertaining and Historical

- Magazines and Books Ephemera
- Music Timeline Ephemera
- Sports, Toys, and Games Ephemera
- Collectability of Movies and Theatre
- Trading Cards and Baseball Cards through the Years

Understanding Ephemera Categories Part One

When you start collecting ephemera, there are several categories of paper items to select from. This is the fun part! You can choose a variety of ephemera items to collect or focus on just one. These ephemera categories are for those with a fondness for history and entertaining pieces.

Tip 14: Magazine Ephemera

Magazine ephemera spans a variety of topics. Collectors can choose a specific type of magazine. Some of those subjects include cars, movies, art, sports, animals, fashion, health, business, and cooking. Check estate sales, yard sales, and used bookstores for magazines that are no longer in print, such as Boing Boing, Ainslee's Magazine, The Class Struggle, Datamation, The Magazine of American History, Town, Ballyhoo, and Nova. Magazines with celebrities on the cover have a higher value. They are also considered cross-collectible. For example, ephemera collectors and sports collectors would want a football magazine. Fashion collectors would also want a fashion magazine.

The first magazine was published in Germany in 1663. The first magazine published in America was "Andrew Bradford's American

Magazine" debuting in 1741. The Illustrated London News was first published in 1852 and was the first magazine to include illustrations. Godey's Lady's Book was first printed in 1830 by Louise Antoine Godey for the purpose of educating American women. Then there are bookazines! A bookazine is a soft-covered book that is of the same size and design as a magazine.

Tip 15: Ephemera Books

An Erratum Slip was a sheet of paper included inside of books that noted any errors in the text that were spotted after the books were published. Addenda Slips are sheets of paper inside books that provide additional information. Under this ephemera category are also bookplates, book covers (dust jackets), and card catalog cards. Borrowers' cards are small cards in the form of pockets that contain details of the library and the date the borrower needs to return the book. Booklets are small books (of up to 35 pages) that are glued, stapled, or sewn together.

There are some books that are considered ephemera pieces, including manuscripts, dime books, chapbooks, penny dreadfuls, blue books, almanacs, comic books, and directories. Chapbooks are one of the earliest forms of books. They were first printed in the 1500s and earned their name because they were sold by peddlers, known as "chapman." Chapbooks are between 10-30 pages and cost between $2-4. Penny Dreadfuls were introduced in 1830. These serial novels included adventure, crime, and sometimes romance; they were often sometimes vicious and violent stories. Dime store novels were paperback books that were approximately 100 pages long. The first dime store novel was published in New York, in 1860, by Beadle and Adams.

Flipbooks are illustrations bound together in a small format book that creates an animated scene when the pages are flipped in rapid succession. They were invented by Pierre-Hubert Desvignes in 1860. But it was John Barnes Linnett who patented the flip book in 1868.

George Coy published the first telephone directory in January 1878. It was a piece of cardboard-like material that held the names and phone numbers of 50 individuals and businesses. There were no phone numbers included in the directory. They did not feel that was necessary. Since many did not own a phone, it was easy for the operator to remember the numbers to connect their calls. Nine months later, as more people brought telephones into their homes, Coy released a new directory called the "telephone book." It was a pamphlet that contained 40 pages. This time it also included the phone numbers. The Donnelly Company introduced the Yellow Pages in 1886.

Almanacs are paperback books that include valuable information, a calendar, statistical information, and sometimes jokes and stories. The first almanac was published in the 1400s. The World Almanac and Book of Facts was published from 1868-1876. It was not published again until 1886. It is still published today. A few of the almanacs that are still published are Grier's Almanac, Astronomical Almanac, and Gray's Sports Almanac made popular from Back to the Future.

The most sought after almanacs are the Farmer's Almanac and the Old Farmer's Almanac. There are a few differences between the two books. The Old Farmer's Almanac was first published in 1792 by Benjamin Franklin. The Farmer's Almanac was published in 1818. The key difference between the two almanacs is their tools and resources for their predictions. The Old Farmer's Almanac makes predictions a year in advance using past weather, solar activity, and solar patterns. The Farmer's Almanac uses tidal activity, sunspot patterns, and the position of the planets to create predictions for two years in advance.

Tip 16: Music Ephemera

Long before television and movies, we had music dating back to the Middle Ages. Today's music ephemera includes songbooks, posters, magazines, album covers, vintage record sleeves, concert tickets, insert cards on CDs and cassettes, and sheet music. Songsters, also called songbooks, were introduced in the 1600s. These paperback books included song lyrics and dance instructions.

Sheet music was first written on clay tablets by Babylonians. After the printing press was invented in the 1400s, sheet music was then produced on paper. When it was first made, sheet music only contained staff lines. The music notes and scribes were added by hand. Carol sheets contain the words only for group singing.

The world's first rock concert, the Moondog Coronation Ball, was held in Cleveland on March 21, 1952. Alan Freed, the father of rock n' roll, organized and hosted the event. The biggest problem of the event – TICKETS! Those little pieces of paper that ephemera collectors treasure so much brought down the first rock concert. Counterfeiters manufactured thousands of replica tickets. On the night of the concert, up to 25,000 tickets were sold for an event that could only hold 10,000 people. An hour after the show started, the crowd grew too big for the building, and the police shut down the show.

Tip 17: The Timeline of Music Genres

In the history of music, there were musicians that led the way for others by launching entirely new platforms. Genres of music all began with a single musician with new ideas. These dates will show you how far back your ephemera collection can go.

The first opera/play was "Dafne" and was written in 1597 by Jacopo Peri. Claudio Monteverdi was the world's first opera singer. He debuted in 1607 with his release of "Orfeo." Today he is considered the Father of Opera.

No one is certain when Blues music began, but Sylvester "Curly" Weaver is credited with creating blues music as we know it today when he released "Guitar Blues and Guitar Rag." William "W.C." Christopher Handy became the Father of the Blues in 1912 when he released "Memphis Blues."

Buddy Bolden First Jazz Musician – Jelly Roll Morton invented jazz when he released "Jelly Roll Blues" in 1915. A year later, Buddy Bolden produced a "looser" form of Roll's music style and became known as the Father of Jazz.

In 1922, Eck Robertson became the first Country musician when he released "Arkansas Traveler" and "Sallie Gooden." Jimmie Rodgers released "Blue Yodel" in 1928 and became the Father of Country Music.

Jackie Brenston & His Delta Cats became the first rock n' roll group in 1951 when they released "Rocket 88." Chuck Berry released "Maybellene" in 1955 and became known as the Father of Rock and Roll.

Led Zeppelin became the first Heavy Metal band when they made their debut album in 1969. They were followed a year later by Black Sabbath and Deep Purple. They became known as the "unholy trinity."

There is a debate over who invented Rap music. Some believe it was DJ Kool Herc. He created rap using two records simultaneously to "isolate and repeat music breaks" while speaking in rhyme. His first song, "Apache," was released in 1975. Still, some believe the first rap musicians were The Fatback Band in 1979 with their song, "King Tim III."

Tip 18: Television, Theatre, and Movies

In the world of television, movies, and theatre, there are plenty of ephemera options to add to your collection. These include posters, cast lists, playbills, programs, ticket stubs, advertisements, photos, and magazines. In addition, a pressbook is a booklet assembled for movie theaters that guides them on how to promote certain films.

Lobby cards were introduced in 1913. These are the movie versions of today's movie poster. They were photographs from scenes in the movie that were printed on a type of cardboard. They were given to movie theaters by production companies in sets of 4, 8, and 12.

They served as advertisements for new movies. When they were first released, they were 8" x 10" in size. In 1913, they were 11" x 14" in size. They stopped making lobby cards in the early 1980s.

Theatre dates back to Acropolis, Athens, during the 5th century. The first theatre was the Theatre of Dionysus. In 1752, Shakespeare's, The Merchant of Venice was performed in Williamsburg, Virginia. This was the first theatrical play held in America. Playbills were first used in the 1700s. Theatre programs were introduced in the 1800s. Theatre was banned in America from 1774 to 1789 because it was deemed immoral.

Louis Le Prince recorded the first motion picture in 1888. His film, Roundhay Garden Scene, was two seconds long. Lumière brothers developed Cinématographe in 1895. This is the concept of developing movies for an audience. His invention changed the entertainment industry forever. After that, movies grew to include sound, color, and eventually CGI.

Philo Taylor Farnsworth developed the first television and demonstrated the TV to the public on September 7, 1927. The first television sets were sold at the New York World's fair in 1939. However, it was not until the 1950s that the TV set became a common fixture in homes. The first tv show was The Queen's Messenger. It first aired on September 11, 1928. The first cartoon, Crusader Rabbit, aired on August 1, 1949. Finally, the first commercial aired in 1941 and was for the Bulova Watch Company. Today, ephemera can be found that celebrates all 3 of these historical moments.

Tip 19: Posters, Photographs, and Stereoview Cards

Stereographs, also known as stereoview cards and stereoscopes, were invented in 1838 by Charles Wheatstone. These are cards that hold two photographs side-by-side that, when viewed through a stereoscope, take on the look of a 3D image. William Brewster invented the handheld stereoscope in 1850.

When lithography was invented in 1798, it aided the process of making posters. Before that, manufacturing posters was slow and expensive, so not many were made. Colored posters were introduced in 1837 after chromolithography was developed. In 1866, Jules Cheret created the first modern poster. He went on to design more than 1,200 more posters. Today he is considered the father of the modern poster. The years 1880-1895 are considered the "birth of the lithographic poster." The first movie poster was for the film "This Gun for Hire." It was produced on December 26, 1895. Before TV and radio, the main source for advertising were posters.

The first photograph was developed in 1826 by Joseph Nicéphore. He titled the photo "View from the Window at Le Gras." William Henry Fox Talbot of Great Britain invented paper photographs in 1839. Salt was the key component in making paper photos. American inventor, Edwin Land, invented the Polaroid instant camera in 1947.

Carte de Visites were created by André Adolphe Eugène Disdéri in 1854. They were small photographs mounted on a form of cardboard the size of a visiting card (4 1/2" x 2 1/2"). This is how they got their name – carte de visite.

Cabinet cards were small cards with photos mounted on the front manufactured from 1866-1914. Photography is one of the greatest inventions. It allowed people to truly capture moments and people's images that they never wanted to forget. As a result, vintage photographs are sought after by both history collectors and ephemera collectors.

Tip 20: Military and Historical Ephemera

Military and historical ephemera includes military documents, letters and postcards written by soldiers, battle orders, and maps used by military troops. Other types include charts, newspapers, notes, pamphlets, flyers, posters, photos, certificates, and ID cards. In 1775, as the "United Colonies" (soon to be the United States) fought for their independence from England, the new nation was officially establishing its armed forces. The US Army was established on June 14, 1775, as the "main ground force" of the military. The Continental Navy was established on October 13, 1775, to protect and "maintain the freedom of the seas." They were disbanded in 1785. Due to the increased illegal activity of Pirates, they were resurrected in 1794 and renamed the United States Navy. The Marines were founded on November 10, 1775, to "specialize in amphibious operations."

It was 15 years later, on August 4, 1790, that the Coast Guard was established. They include ships, boats, aircraft, and shore stations that conduct a variety of missions. The United States Merchant Marines was launched on March 15, 1938, to carry out several roles. During times of peace, they transport cargo and passengers. During times of war, they are "an auxiliary to the United States Navy and can be called upon to deliver military personnel and materiel for the military." Finally, the Air Force was established on September 18, 1947. Before that, they were a section of the Army known as the Army Air Corps. The role of the Air Force is to "defend the United States through exploitation through air and space."

Draft cards are also a part of military ephemera. The draft was established after the start of World War I. Before World War II, the swastika was worn as a patch on the left shoulder of the 45th Infantry Division to honor Native Americans. The swastika was replaced by a gold-colored eagle. On March 13, 1942, the U.S. Army launched the K-9 Corps. The marines adopted the bulldog as their mascot in 1924. Uncle Sam was introduced on Army recruiting posters in 1917; James Montgomery Flagg designed the poster. The name Uncle Sam was derived from Samuel Wilson, a meat packer who supplied rations for soldiers during the War of 1812. After the war, people started associating Uncle Sam with anything related to the United States.

Tip 21: Holidays and Greeting Cards

The first greeting cards were printed on papyrus in Germany in 1400. The first holiday cards were made for Valentine's Day cards. They were first made in the 1700s. In 1849, Esther Howland became one of the largest producers of Valentine cards in America. Christmas cards were introduced in 1843 by Henry Cole; he had the card designed by artist John Calcott Horsley. In 1846, Louis Prang brought the Christmas cards to America. He was working as a printer in Boston. He later became known as the "Father of the American Christmas card." Birthday cards also made their debut in the mid-1800s. Concertina cards are greeting cards that fold and open in a layer fashion, similar to an accordion.

In 1949, Esther Howland opened the first greeting card publishing company in America. American Greetings was founded in 1906 by Jacob Sapirstein; other greeting card makers include Avanti Press, Inklings Paperie, Red Oak Letterpress, and Elum Designs.

Joyce Clyde "JC" Hall established the Hallmark company in 1910 when he was only 18 years old. Having just arrived in Kansas City, Missouri, he was living out of a room at the YMCA. He had two shoeboxes filled with postcards and was selling them through a mail order business he started. A year later, he and his brothers, Rollie and William, named the company Hall Brothers. In 1912, they expanded their product line to include greeting cards. Then, in 1914, they started making their own line of cards.

The Greeting Card Association was established in 1941. Each year, they distribute the LOUIE Award to greeting card designers.

Tip 22: Political Ephemera

Political ephemera includes fliers, letters, posters, personal documents, clippings, pamphlets, broadsides, ballots, election manifestos, newsletters, and bumper stickers. Topics covered in political ephemera include campaigns, petitions, land rights movements, conservation, peace movements, elections, women's movements, and racism.

The word "gerrymandering" was first used on a political broadside. It was in 1812 when the Jeffersonian Republicans pushed a bill through the Massachusetts legislature requesting the district lines be redrawn in a way that would, coincidentally, give him the advantage in the upcoming election. The lines were almost drawn into the shape of a salamander, which was, at the time, a mythological lizard. They were actually alive during the Jurassic period. The governor, Elbridge Gerry, signed the bill, agreeing to the redistricting request. The image that looked like the mythical salamander was nicknamed the "Gerry-mander," a new species of monster. Today, "gerrymander" is defined as "manipulating the boundaries to favor one party or class."

The University of Chicago Library houses a large collection of political ephemera dating from 1939-1950. This is known as the American Reactionary Political Ephemera Collection. Topics that are covered in the collection include "anti-Semitism, communism, isolationism, nationalism, racism, fascism, and other issues related to ultraconservative social, religious, and economic movements."

Tip 23: Trade/Trading Cards Through the Years

Trading cards, also known as trade cards, were introduced in 1670 and were used as advertisements. Some of the cards included maps to the store where the products could be bought. Trade cards were first circulated in Paris and England. In 1850, Aristide Boucicaut of Paris added color to trading cards. In the mid-1850s, Louis Prang, Christmas card designer, introduced the first "album cards." They were a set of cards sold on a single sheet. Some collectors cut the sheet into single cards, but many kept them intact.

Shipper cards were trading cards that announced the sailing schedules of clipper ships. They were made from 1853 to the 1860s. Companies that sold tea bags throughout the 1950s and 1960s also included trading cards in their boxes called tea cards. Some of these tea companies were Cooper (1961), Typhoo (1903), Brooke Bond Red Label (1903), Cooper (1961), Red Rose (1894), and Lipton (1871). The tea cards came filled with educational facts on subjects, including flags of the world, wildflowers, butterflies, birds, ships, dinosaurs, and transportation history. In 1986, Eclipse Comics printed a line of trading cards from 1989-1993 that covered politics, true crime, and organized crime.

Baseball trading cards were introduced in 1865 and were the creation of Charles H Williamson of Brooklyn, New York. The first baseball card featured the Brooklyn Atlantics and was passed out to fans at baseball games.

In 1866, when Andrew Peck and Irving Snyder founded the Peck & Snyder Company of New York, they produced rubber-soled tennis shoes and sports equipment. That year, they also became the first company to manufacture baseball cards. Fleer started making their cards in 1885. Topps started producing baseball cards in 1938; Donruss followed in 1954, and Upper Deck debuted their cards in 1988.

In 1886, baseball cards Old Judge cigarettes started including baseball cards in their cigarette packs. The thickness of the cards gave added protection to the cigarettes. In 1895, W.D. & H.O. Wills, a tobacco company in England, introduced cigarette cards, also known as "tobacco cards." Their first set of cards featured "Ships & Soldiers." Two years later, in 1897, they released the "Kings & Queens" series.

In the early 1930s, baseball cards were sold in packs with a stick of pink bubble gum. This was done more to promote the bubble gum. It was the Fleer Company (Dubble Bubble) and the Goudey Gum Company that started the trend of including baseball cards to entice buyers to purchase their gum.

Sports ephemera includes more than just baseball cards. There are racing bibs, sports posters, photographs, newspaper clippings, betting slips, football polls, almanacs, die cuts, magazines, schedules, and autographs. Scott Sports introduced the first racing bibs in Europe in 1958. They were first worn by competitors in America in 1973 for the Carlsbad 500cc Grand Prix. Today people try to wear numbers on their racing bibs that are significant to them, such as lucky numbers, birthdays, or anniversaries.

There are a variety of ephemera toys and games to add to your collection. They include play money, Bingo cards, kites, Beetle Drive cards, scavenger hunt lists, paper soldiers, Jumping Jacks, puppets, puzzles, coloring books, activity books, puzzle cards, and paper dolls. Ephemera pieces for board games are also collectible.

These include game cards (Candyland, Monopoly, Trivial Pursuit, Uncle Wiggly Game cards), score sheets, and instruction books. Paper bowling games were first manufactured in the late 1800s. You can also add paper toys that we played with as children, such as paper airplanes, paper footballs, and fortune tellers (also known as a cootie catcher or chatterbox).

Though Bingo games date back to 1530, Edwin Lowe created modern Bingo cards in 1929. As a result, paper Bingo cards are known as "throwaways."

The McLoughlin Brothers, with illustrator Kate Greenaway, created the first coloring book in 1880. Greenaway's coloring book, The Little Folks' Painting Book, included a nursery rhyme with each illustration.

Milton Bradley introduced play money in 1880. It was meant for educational purposes and was passed out to kindergarten classrooms for free. In 1935 they introduced the board game, Easy Money. This was the first board game to include play money. Today, Monopoly money is the most popular version of play money.

Paper dolls got their start in France in the 1700s and were originally called "Pantins." Before children played with them, they were used by adults for the fun of mocking the wealthy. That changed in 1810 when SJ Fuller of London released "The History and Adventures of Little Henry." This was the first set of paper dolls manufactured as a toy for children. The company's most popular paper doll was Little Fanny. In 1828, the McLoughlin Brothers redesigned paper dolls from being jointed figures to having tabs. This also allowed children to change their clothes. The McLoughlin Brothers grew to be one of the largest manufacturers of paper dolls. Their most popular paper dolls were Lottie Love and Dottie Dimple. When Godey's Lady Book magazine debuted in 1830, it included a page of paper dolls. They were the first magazine to do this. They were followed by newspapers that started including a sheet of paper dolls in the Sunday section. As paper dolls grew in demand, department stores started using them to promote and advertise merchandise sold in their stores.

Tip 25: Zoos, Animal Parks, and Animal Ephemera

A lot of ephemera collectors focus on their favorite animals – penguins, tigers, elephants, and even dinosaurs. However, for frog enthusiasts, there is a line of ephemera titled "Frog in Your Throat." The company made cough drops and cough syrup in the 1800s. Ephemera items that featured their famous frog promoting their Frog in Your Throat cough drops include advertisements, wrappers, postcards, medicine cards, labels, and boxes.

Queen Hatshepsut opened the first zoo in Egypt in 1500 BC. She collected animals from across Africa and invited the public to tour the grounds and see the animals in her collection. Paris, France, was the site of the first modern zoo. The Philadelphia Zoo was the first zoo to open in America. They opened in 1874 and are still open today. The Central Park Zoo opened five years later. Photos, postcards, brochures, posters, and food wrappers are just a few types of animal ephemera that can be collected from animal parks across the country.

In 1964, David DeMott, George Millay, Ken Norris, and Milt Shedd collaborated to open an underwater restaurant. However, after a few changes to their project, the result was the first SeaWorld!

Tip 26: Entertainment Ephemera

Entertainment ephemera includes posters, invitations, decorations, tickets, flyers, bill sides, stickers, newspaper articles, guest lists, paper flags, paper flowers, napkins, and even snack wrappers. These items promote carnivals, fairs, amusement parks, and magic shows. Richard Potter was the first magician from America and the first to perform shows on stage. He started his career in 1811. Jean Eugene Robert-Houdin opened the first magic theatre in Paris in 1845 and is considered to be the Father of Magic.

The concept of fairs dates back to biblical days and is even mentioned in the Bible. In 1765, in York, Pennsylvania, the first fair was held in America, in the location now known as Penn Park. This was when fairs began to transform into modern fairs as we know them. There were displays of farm animals and agricultural supplies, along with activities for children to make it a family event. The Berkshire County Fair was the first modern fair in America, including food booths, rides, games, and contests; it was organized in 1807 by Franklin Watson. The fair was held in Pittsfield, Massachusetts. The town still holds that fair every year. In 1841, New York held the first state fair. Britain held the first World's Fair in 1851. Philadelphia, Pennsylvania hosted the first World's Fair in America in 1876; it was held in celebration of America's centennial celebration. The key difference between a carnival and a fair is that a carnival includes shows.

Chapter 3: Ephemera Categories ~ Everyday Ephemera

- Following Advertisements
- Food and Beverage Labels
- Understanding Paper Money
- The World of Travel and Communications Ephemera
- Stamps (America's Favorite Collectible)

Understanding Ephemera Categories Part Two

These ephemera categories cover "everyday" ephemera that is around us all the time. We use paper products in so many ways that collectors found it easier to make these categories to classify ephemera when storing, sharing, buying, and selling.

Tip 27: Advertisements and Promotional Ephemera

Broadsides and flyers were the first types of advertising ephemera. In the 1800s, ads began to be printed on all types of items, including calendars, trade cards, matchbooks, postcards, maps, menus, theater programs, and envelopes. Matchbooks were introduced in 1892. Pabst Blue Ribbon became the first company to advertise on matchbooks in 1894. Daniel Defoe published the first newspaper ad on May 8, 1704. The ad ran in the Boston News-Letter and was for property for sale on Oyster Bay, Long Island. The New York Ledger ran the first full-page ad in 1856.

The Tiffany Blue Book catalog was first printed in 1845. This was the first mail order catalog in the United States. The Montgomery Ward catalog was introduced in 1872, and the first Sears Christmas catalog was published in 1933. It was 78 pages and included items such as the Miss Pigtails doll, a Mickey Mouse watch, electric trains, live singing canaries, fruitcakes, and a 5-pound box of chocolates. The catalog was promoted as the Wish Book. Showcards are advertisements on cards that are placed on countertops or in a window.

Tip 28: Office, Industry, and Business Ephemera

Stationery, envelopes, letterheads, business documents, and contracts are all types of office ephemera. Industry ephemera are paper items associated with machinery used in businesses, such as factories, dump trucks, cranes, and other large machines; this type of ephemera includes workbooks, manuals, posters, newspapers, magazines, and even greeting cards. Legal ephemera includes contracts, affidavits, wills, appeals, and jury lists. Waybills are business documents that are used to keep a record of goods carried on tractor trailers, ships, and trains. Finally, certificates include marriage certificates, civil partnership certificates, birth certificates, stock certificates, and those given as awards for achievements. These paper items are considered to be Business Ephemera:

- Ledgers
- Awards
- Checks
- Brochures
- Receipts
- Business Cards
- Advertisements
- Blueprints
- Documents
- Contracts
- Trade Cards
- Sales Material
- Banking Documents
- Promotional Items
- Bearer Bonds
- Savings Bonds

Envelopes were invented in 1840; before that, writers used "letter sheets." These were single sheets of paper that could be written on and then folded in a way that the writing was covered so it could be shipped out. Other types of envelopes are advertising envelopes and coin envelopes. Crash covers are envelopes that were recovered from train and airplane accidents.

Business cards were first made in China during the 1400s and were called "Visitor Cards." During the Victorian Era, they were known as "calling cards." People would put fun and interesting information about themselves and leave them at people's homes after they visited them. This was mainly done when someone visited another person, but they were not home. They were also passed out as a means to introduce themselves. They were brought to America in the mid-1800s and used until the early 1900s. It was considered proper etiquette to pass out calling cards when visiting people. Some men used these to introduce themselves to women when they were looking for someone to court. They were known as acquaintance cards. Today these calling cards, now known as business cards, are divided into three categories: Exclusive Business Cards, Premium Business Cards, and Standard Business Cards. What category they fall in depends on the quality of paper that is used.

There are many more types of cards that ephemera collectors seek. Private view cards are invitations sent out to invite people to a private viewing at an art exhibition. Know the difference between escort cards and seat cards. The escort cards show guests the table they are placed at, and the seat cards tell them which chair is theirs at that table. Calling cards are also called prostitute cards, naughty cards, and hooker cards. Ham Radio cards and Dance cards are also collectible ephemera pieces.

Tip 29: Ephemera Labels

Many ephemera collectors are fond of labels. The fruit crate labels are the most popular. Other types of ephemera labels are wine labels, banana labels, beer labels, hot sauce labels, cigar labels, and vintage prescription labels. Unfortunately, mistakes have been found on some labels. These can include the wrong details or names, missing information, or the wrong color.

Alcohol labels can include beer, whisky, and wine. One of the earliest types of labels was found on wine bottles that date back to 1550 in Egypt. However, labels were not applied to beer bottles until the mid-1800s.

Banana labels were first used in 1930 by Meloripe. Elders & Fyffes of the UK started putting labels on their fruit in 1929. These are known as "Fyffes Blue Labels." The Boston Fruit Company was opened in 1885 by Andrew Preston and Lorenzo Baker. The United Fruit Company was established in 1899 after the Boston Fruit Company merged with Minor C Keith, one of the world's largest banana growers. The United Fruit Company made fruit labels that are most sought after.

Poster stamps were introduced in 1864. They are similar to labels and are slightly larger than a postage stamp. They first depicted images from popular posters. Topics of poster stamps later included military, flags, artwork, advertising, and politics.

Labels also include fish crate labels, gunmakers' labels, canned food labels, shaker labels, railway & carriage window labels, and back labels (found on wine bottles). Bale labels were paper tags produced by the textile industry from 1890 to 1974. They were attached to the outside of bales of fabric and sometimes between the layers.

Tip 30: Collectability of Stickers

Stickers also fall under the category of labels. Historians believe stickers date back to early Egypt after archaeologists discovered paper that was stuck to the walls in ancient Egyptian buildings. Stickers were manufactured again after 1796 with the invention of lithography. These stickers had glue on the back and needed to be dabbed with water to make them sticky. Then, in 1935, Ray Stanton Avery developed modern stickers with the self-adhesive backs as we know them today.

In the late 1940s, Forest Gill created the first bumper sticker. Giuseppe Panini teamed with FIFA in 1970 and manufactured the first sticker albums boosting the popularity of collecting stickers. In 1965, Gale Matson of the 3M Company was trying to invent a type of carbonless paper when he "accidentally" invented scratch and sniff stickers. Creative Teaching Press was a popular maker of scratch and sniff stickers in 1977.

Tip 31: Mourning Ephemera

Memorial cards also were introduced in Europe in the 1700s and were first known as Mourning cards. They were first produced as trade cards. Envelopes with black lines drawn around the border and edges were called "mourning covers." At first, the black lines would be drawn thick. As time went on, the black line was made thinner. In 1860, the New York Herald coined the word "morgue." They were also the first newspaper to include an obituary section. Pallbearer cards, death notices, suicide notes, and obituaries are all examples of mourning and memorial ephemera.

Cemetery plans are diagrams that indicate the locations of graves in a cemetery. Then there are "cemetery cards" issued by cemeteries to help visitors locate specific grave plots.

Tip 32: Bank Notes and Paper Money Ephemera

Bank notes were promissory notes issued by banks or given to merchants as a promise to pay for goods and services. Paper money was first used in China in 806 A.D. However, it was not widely used until 1000 A.D. Europe started using paper money in 1661. Paper money was introduced in the United States on February 3, 1690, and was called "colonial currency." It was produced from 1690-1774.

Following the Revolutionary War, paper money was referred to as "continental currency." Each state created its own currency amounts and printed its own paper money. This started causing confusion among the states when people tried to use the money in states outside of the one that printed the money. Another problem arrived when so much money was printed that it caused rapid inflation. So in 1787, congress stopped letting states produce their own form of currency and started creating money in one set of style and currency values to be used by the entire nation.

In 1861, the United States government introduced the five-, ten-, and twenty-dollar bills. The one was introduced in 1862 and had Samuel Chase on the front. George Washington replaced him in 1869. The two-dollar bill was also introduced in March 1862 and featured Alexander Hamilton. Paper money was produced after 1862 and called "Greenbacks."

Tip 33: Newspapers and Broadsides

Broadsides are larger-sized sheets of paper that were only printed on one side. They were first used to carry information on disasters, crimes, and executions. They later served as advertisements and also for politicians during elections. They became popular in 1796 when Alois Senefelder invented the process of lithography. He was looking for a less expensive method of making engravings on metal plates. His new "broadsides" entailed making drawings and engravings on Bavarian limestone using a greasy crayon and then transferring that image onto paper. Broadsides were also used for posting school and business rules, ballads, WANTED posters, "lost" posters, entertainment schedules, and notices.

The Acta Diurna was the very first newspaper and was printed in Rome in 59 BC. The Notizie Scritte was the first monthly newspaper. It was printed in Venice in 1556. Antwerp (Belgium) published the first weekly newspaper, "Relation," in 1605. London introduced the Daily Courant in 1621. This was the first daily newspaper and debuted on March 11, 1702. The first American newspaper, the Boston News Letter, was printed in 1705. The Pennsylvania Packet and Daily Advertiser was the first daily newspaper in America. It was printed from September 21, 1784 -

December 31, 1790. Underground newspapers are also referred to as Clandestine Newspapers.

The New York Sun newspaper was published from 1833-1950. When it debuted, it only cost one cent. Newspapers followed them and lowered their price to a penny. This was known as the beginning of the "penny press." The Washington Post newspaper brought the penny press to an end in 1877 when it raised its price to 3 cents.

Tip 34: Tickets and Trading Stamps

For your ephemera collection, include these types of tickets: scratch tickets, lottery tickets, tickets to events, sports, and concerts, and then airline, train, and bus tickets. In 1934, the lottery was introduced in Puerto Rico. Trade stamps from England were known as "Green Shield Stamps."

In 1891, Schuster's Department Store in Wisconsin became the first business to offer the concept of trading stamps as a loyalty program for their customers. The most popular of these trading stamps were the S&H Green Stamps. They were introduced in 1896 by Sperry & Hutchinson and distributed until the 1980s. After that, A&P stores passed out MacDonald Plaid Stamps. In Texas, H-E-B grocery stores passed out Texas Gold Stamps. Grocery stores in Hawaii passed out Mahalo Stamps. Other types of trading stamps were Blue Chip Stamps, Triple S Blue Stamps, Valu-Plus, Gold Strike Stamps, Top Value Stamps, Gold Bond Stamps, Quality Stamps, Buccaneer Stamps, King Korn stamps, and Gold Bond Stamps.

College stamps were used by Oxford and Cambridge Universities, from 1871 to 1886, for internal mail. Lecture lists and lecture tickets fall under the categories of both college and business ephemera.

On August 28, 1941, President Roosevelt signed an executive order that issued ration cards to American families. Each book included sheets of stamps that could be used for coffee, meat, canned goods, cooking oil, and sugar. Due to the war, stores were lacking in those items, and ration stamps allowed each family to get these necessary goods. In addition, by putting a limit on how much they could get, it allowed for there to be enough for everyone. Today, collectors sell ration stamps for $5-$10. Many of these ration stamps are on display at the National World War II Museum.

Tip 35: Travel and Communications Ephemera

Travel and communications ephemera include postcards, maps, travel guides, brochures, advertisements, timetables, stamps, hotel stationery, travel tickets, letters, luggage tags, telegrams, and pamphlets. Envelopes with illustrations drawn on the front are known as "mail art." It was common for soldiers to decorate their envelopes with drawings. Luggage tags were introduced in 1900 and grew in popularity in the 1960s. Tide tables are often used by ship captains. When an airline is found to be properly registered and passes inspection to be deemed safe for flight, they receive an "airworthiness certificate." These also make great additions to your collection.

Here are more "first moments" to remember when collecting Travel and Communication Ephemera. John Murray of London, England, published the first travel guides in 1836 under the name "Murray's Handbooks for Travellers."

Samuel Morse, the inventor of the telegraph, sent the first telegraphic message on May 24, 1844, from Washington DC to Baltimore. The telegraph contained the words: What hath God wrought! The words were taken from Numbers 23:23. The first transatlantic telegram was sent on August 16, 1858. The Atlantic Telegraph Company got its start in 1866. The message read: "Glory to God in the highest; on earth, peace and good will to all men."

Airmail is different than telegrams. This is mail carried from one location to another by airplane or helicopter. There are several forms of ephemera related to airmail, including airgraph forms (stationery), envelopes, covers, and labels.

Timetables are schedules that show the arrival and departure times of trolleys (trams), airships, ferries and boats, buses, trains, and airplanes. The website www.timetableimages.com is comprised of two sections. One is devoted to collecting airline timetables, and the other is for maritime timetables. Both include information on airline/shipping companies and a list of airlines/ships. In addition, the airline timetable page includes an index of airline baggage labels.

Some of the makers of paper maps are Benchmark Maps, Rand McNally, and Michelin Travel. Styles of maps include road maps, city maps, subway maps, fish and game maps, bus route maps, cycle maps show, escape maps, subway maps, tourist maps, national parks, and forest maps, and amusement park maps. Even stores and malls developed maps of the inside of their buildings.

Tip: 36 Origin of Postcards

Demaison of Paris, France, created the first postcards in 1777. However, people were worried that others would read their messages, so they would not use them. Emanuel Herrmann re-invented the postcard on October 1, 1869. With his design, there was a place on the back for the message, and on the front, there was a place for the address, and a stamp was included in the corner. In the 1880s, small designs were included on the front of postcards. Modern postcards that included a full image on one side were introduced in 1893 at the World's Columbian Exposition by Charles Goldsmith. This was also the first time they were sold in America. The years between 1898 – 1919 are considered the Golden Age of Postcards.

Picture postcards made between 1901 – 1906 are undivided on the back. Postcards printed between 1907 – 1919 are divided on the back, and a white border was added to postcards made between 1915 – 1930.

Tip 37: Patterns and Paper Fashions

The Scott Paper Company introduced the first paper dresses in 1966. They sold for $1, and the fabric was similar to the bibs worn at the dentist's office. Paper dresses were then made for children, and for the boys, there were paper overalls. There were also paper wedding gowns and paper wedding dresses. For men, there were paper shirts, pants, vets, and suits.

Another type of paper fashion for ephemera collectors is patterns that were sold for people to make their own clothes. Ellen Curtis Demorest started them in 1860. The McCall Pattern Company made the most popular of these; they were first produced in 1919. The company started printing instructions directly on the pattern in 1920. Before that, the instructions were printed on a separate sheet of paper. Some tea cards also included patterns. Other types of paper fashion include illustrations, paper slippers, headpieces& hats, and paper fans. There are also patterns for knitting, needlepoint, shoe patterns, and cross stitch.

Tip 38: Old School Ephemera

Schoolhouse ephemera includes old report cards, flashcards, teacher's work papers, workbooks, quiz sheets & test papers, certificates and awards, alphabet sheets, detention cards, school newspapers, lesson plans, and bookmarks. The first bookmarks were introduced in 500 AD and made of leather. Paper bookmarks were first created in 1584 by Christopher Barker.

The first schools focused on three subjects: reading, writing, and arithmetic (math). The first public school in the United States opened in Boston, Massachusetts, on April 23, 1635. At that time, children were needed at home during the farming season to help with the work of planting and harvesting crops, which was done in spring, summer, and fall. As a result, the school year was scheduled in a way that gave those months off, a trend that stayed long after children were expected to be home and assist with farming work. This is why there is no school in June, July, and August.

In 1785, Yale started the concept of awarding 100 points as a perfect score. In the mid-1800s. This was the first grading scale used by schools. In 1792, William Farish created the system of giving grades (A-F) to students. He was a tutor at Cambridge University and felt the grades would give him a better idea of what help the students needed. This grading system was brought to the United States in the late 1800s. In the early 1900s, they added percentage grades to letter grades. Knowing the timeline of school grades will help collectors determine the age of school ephemera.

Dartmouth University published the first school newspaper. Their newspaper, the Dartmouth Gazette, was first published on August 27, 1799, and is still printed today. Phillips Academy printed the first high school newspaper in 1857. Their newspaper, the Phillipian, was first published on July 28, 1857.

Flashcards were the creation of Favell Lee Mortimer in 1834. She was an English teacher and created flashcards as an easier way to teach her students how to read. French occultist, Jean-Baptiste Alliette, invented Tarot cards in 1785.

In 1976, Mead introduced a line of Critter Sitter's characters for their notebooks. They were beloved by students and now by collectors. These chubby-cheeked animals were also put on puzzles, notebook pads, pocket folders, napkins, and stickers.

Tip 39: Food and Beverage Ephemera

When collecting food and beverage ephemera, you can include labels, advertisements, recipe cards, paperback cookbooks, meal plans, signs, posters, bags and wrappers, newspaper clippings, and magazines. Cutlery pockets are paper or cardboard pockets used to carry silverware to tables in restaurants. In addition, you can collect food vouchers, cloakroom tickets, wine lists, menus, restaurant placemats, and beermats from restaurants.

The first modern cookbook was the Boston Cooking-School Cookbook. It was written in 1896 by Fannie Farmer and was over 600 pages. Along with recipes, it included helpful tips, cooking definitions, food values, and instructions for canning and drying fruits and vegetables. Fannie Farmer was a leader in the field of cooking. She started cooking when she was a student at the Boston Cooking School. After she graduated, she was hired as an assistant to the director and later the principal. She established several concepts that would change the way people follow recipes and cook. Her first development was to design the standard set of measuring spoons and measuring cups that we use today. She also changed the format for recipes in a way that listed the ingredients first, with precise measurements, followed by the directions that were listed in order. These concepts were all included in her cookbook. Before this, recipes were listed in paragraph form.

In 1862, President Lincoln established the Department of Agriculture and the Bureau of Chemistry. In 1940, its name was changed to the Food and Drug Administration (FDA). They made several changes to food packages through the years. They started listing ingredients in 1940 and added sterilization labels in 1957. In 1973, the USDA made it mandatory for companies to include nutrition information to be added to labels. This also marked the first year food products were labeled "organic." That same year, some of the first products were labeled "organic."

In 1856, the National Biscuit Co. (NABISCO) became the first company to sell a product (Oyster Crackers) wrapped in packaging designed with their name and product details. The Wardlow-Thomas Paper Company made the packaging for NABISCO. In 1906, Kellogg's released the first cereal box. It was for their toasted corn flakes.

Tip: 40 Timeline of Cereal Ephemera

A popular subject under food ephemera is cereal! This includes cereal boxes, signs, posters & wall art, both vintage, and current advertisements, and even cereal coupons. Vintage cereal advertisements are cross-collectible and highly sought after by collectors of ephemera, cereal, and advertisements.

Granula was the first breakfast cereal created by Dr. James Caleb Jackson in 1863. The cereal had to soak in milk overnight before it could be eaten and was called "wheat rocks." When John Kellogg produced his own version of the cereal in 1881, he renamed it "Granola" and manufactured it in the form of flakes so that it could be eaten right away. It was also the first cereal to be sold in a box. Before the creation of the cereal box, stores kept the cereal in a barrel and would scoop it out for sales. To date, over 5,000 brands of cereal have been produced. These cereals are considered antique because they are over 100 years old:

- Wheatena (1879)
- Shredded Wheat (1890)
- Granose Flakes (1895)
- Vitos (Wheat Cereal) (1897)
- Grape-Nuts (1897)
- Corn Flakes (1898)
- Force (wheat flakes) (1901)
- Puffed Rice (1901)
- Wheat Berry Flakes (1908)
- Krumbles (1912)

The 1950s is considered the Golden Age of Cereal. Some of America's favorite cereal was introduced in that decade. We can thank the Golden Age of Cereal for these favorites. Cereal advertisements are interesting due to their curious words to promote cereal. For example, in 1967, Rice Cream Flakes was advertised as a cereal "dipped in freeze-dried real ice cream."

Chapter 4: Ephemera History

- Paper through the Years
- First Moments in the History of Paper
- Stamps (America's Favorite Collectible)
- Timeline of Advertising Mascots
- Highlights of Playing Cards

A History in Ephemera

As with any type of collectible, ephemera has notable pieces that started an entire line of products that continued to expand over the years. Having a "first" will always add value and interest to your collection. Understanding the history of different types of ephemera will help you determine the age and value of each piece. It will also help you avoid being misled into thinking an item is older than it actually is. Not to mention, it makes the collection much more interesting for yourself – and for showing off your paper pieces. Ephemera plays an important role in history. They educate us on moments, events, and lifestyles, all captured on paper.

Tip 41: How It All Began

It all started in 3000 BC when Egyptians created papyrus. This was the first version of paper. In 105 AD, Ts'ai Lun invented modern paper using a mash of products including rags, grass, hemp, fishnets, and mulberry bark. In 500 AD, the Mayans developed a way to make paper by only using tree bark. Europe started printing paper in 1151 AD. Italy created watermarks and started adding them to paper in 1282 AD.

John Tate opened a paper mill in England in 1490. William Rittenhouse brought papermaking to America in 1690. He opened a log mill in Philadelphia and began manufacturing paper. As paper became easier to make, there was a flux in the production of documents, advertisements, and published books.

Johann Gutenberg invented the movable type printing press in 1453. He then published the Bible in 1455. It was the first book published using his invention.

In 1798, Nicolas-Louis Robert invented the first machine that made paper. Henry and Sealy Fourdrinier improved the machine a year later so that it also made paperboard and fiberboard. Finally, in 1804, the first book was printed using Robert's invention.

Tip 42: Understanding Leaflets, Flyers, Brochures, and Pamphlets

Common forms of ephemera are leaflets, flyers, brochures, and pamphlets. However, there are differences among them. Brochures were first printed in 1523 and are advertisements that promote services and products that businesses have to offer. Pamphlets were first printed in 1562 to educate the public on different topics. They have several pages and are sometimes called booklets. Flyers, also known as handbills, have information and images printed on both sides. Leaflets are similar to flyers but are smaller in size, and flyers are used for one-time events.

Tip 43: Ephemera Makers Through the Years

Knowing the biographies of designers and the history of manufacturers will help to date the ephemera pieces and determine their values.

Colonel Daniel Mead teamed with investors to establish the "Ellis, Chaffin & Company" in 1846 in Dayton, Ohio. Mead bought out the original partners in 1856. The company's name changed as he worked with different partners in the years that followed. The company became "Mead and Weston" in 1860 and then switched to

"Weston and Mead" in 1866. In 1873, the name was changed to Mead & Nixon Paper Company. They underwent their final name change under Daniel Mead in 1882 to the Mead Paper Company. In 1891, Daniel Mead passed away and his sons, Charles and Harry, took charge of the company. Due to reckless spending, the company almost went bankrupt. In 1905, investors approached Daniel's son, George, to take control of the company, and he agreed. Under George Mead, the company name was changed to Mead Pulp and Paper Company. They were producing 15 types of paper. In 1921, George expanded and opened the Mead Sales Company only to manufacture white paper. They added paperboard to their line of paper products in 1925, which led to them opening the Mead Paperboard Corporation in 1927.

Brothers E. Irvin Scott and Clarence Scott founded the Scott Paper Company in 1879. the first products they made were paper bags and wrapping paper.

The Columbia River Paper Company was launched in 1884. Their name was changed to the Crown Columbia Paper Co. in 1905. Their first paper products were cigarette packages, gum wrappers, postcards, pickle labels, magazines, tobacco pouches, coffee bags, and paper for books. In 1914, they merged with the Willamette Falls Pulp and Paper Company which first opened on October 7, 1889. Their first product was Zee toilet paper.

Also, in 1884, the Crystal Paper Company opened. The Peerless Paper Company opened in 1898 under the name Peerless Manufacturing Company. Both companies got their start by making toilet paper, paper towels, and napkins. Mead bought Peerless in 1917.

The American Writing Paper Company opened in 1899. They were large producers of printing and writing paper.

The Manistique Pulp and Paper Company opened in 1916. The company went through several ownerships. They were bought by Mead in 1942 and were sold again in 1952 to Kearney. Field Enterprises bought the company in 1960 and changed its name to Manistique Papers, Inc and then to FutureMark Manistique. The company closed in 2015 and was reopened a year later by UP Paper LLC.

Tip 44: Ephemera Firsts

Paper is one of the greatest and most important products in history. There have been several milestones in the history of papermaking. Author Wang Chieh wrote the "Diamond Sutra" in the year 868. This was a 16-foot-long scroll and is considered to be the first book.

Hu Shih wrote the first dictionary in China in 149 BC. Robert Cawdrey wrote the first English dictionary in 1604. China also invented cardboard in the early 1600s. One of the first uses was to line the inside of men's top hats. His book, Robert Cawdrey's Table Alphabeticall, had definitions of 3,000 words. Samuel Johnson modernized the dictionary and taught the importance of having the book. He is considered the Father of the Modern Dictionary.

China invented toilet paper in 875 AD. At the start of the 1800s, they started adding bleach to paper to make it white. Split Fountain Printing is the process that allows printers to use more than one color on paper products. It was developed in the early 1870s. John Mark and Lyman Hollingsworth introduced manila paper in 1843. They named the paper after the manila hemp ropes that were used to make the paper. The first food wrappers were used in 1856 and made from corrugated paper. The Eastern Paper Bag Company introduced paper grocery bags in 1870. Paper towels were invented in 1879. Seth Wheeler invented the cardboard toilet paper core and created the perforated tears on toilet paper in 1891, and paper plates were introduced in 1904. Hershey's made the first chocolate bar wrapper in 1890 for their 'nickel bars.' In 1957, Mead created the paper carrier used for six packs of glass beverage bottles.

The first composition notebook was made in France in 1886 by Jean-Michael Basquiat. The cover featured an actual piece of marble. Roaring Spring Paper Products was the first to start making composition notebooks as we know them today, featuring the same marble look but on a soft cover instead of using real marble. These were known as the Roaring Spring Blank Book.

Tip 45: A History of Stamps

Stamp collecting was the fastest growing collection of ephemera. The first postage stamp was the British Penny Black stamp, released on May 6, 1840. The postage stamp was introduced in 1847. Collectors started saving them in the early 1850s. By 1886, there were approximately 25,000 stamp collectors in the United States. Collectors of stamps then became known as "philatelists." In April 1886, collectors organized the Committee on the National Organization of Philatelists. On September 13, 1886, the group met and decided to change the name to the American Philatelic Association. They elected John Tiffany to be the group's first president the next day. In 1977, they hosted their first annual convention – Stampshow. At their 1995 convention, they introduced Stamp Saturday, an educational program for stamp collectors.

Tip 46: Studying the History of the Circus

The Circus Historical Society was established in 1939 to educate on the history of the circus. Their annual convention extends over three days and includes historical presentations and auctions.

Philip Astley hosted the first modern circus on April 4, 1768. The show included horse riding tricks, clowns, and acrobats. Dan Castello and William Cameron Coup opened Dan Castello's Great Circus & Egyptian Caravan in 1867. In 1871, they merged with PT Barnum's Grand Traveling Museum. On April 10, 1871, Phineas Taylor "PT" Barnum and his partner, James Bailey, opened the curtains to hold their first Barnum and Bailey Circus show. Barnum dubbed their circus "the greatest show on earth." On most occasions, Barnum was a pleasant entertainer. However, he was also a dishonest businessman who coined the phrase, "There's a sucker born every minute." Before the duo opened their circus, Barnum was a publisher for the Herald of Freedom weekly newspaper, where he was arrested three times for libel. The most popular attraction at their circus was Charles Stratton, also known as General Tom Thumb." He was a man that stood 25 inches tall.

The Ringling Brothers, Albert, Otto, Alfred, Charles, and John, opened the Ringling Brothers Circus in 1884. Their first show was held on May 19, 1884. The brothers got their start holding small shows in their backyard when they were children.

Tip 47: Advertising Highlights to Age Your Ephemera

Advertisements make a large part of collecting ephemera. Knowing the history of iconic ads and companies can help you determine the age of the ephemera. This is especially beneficial at times when people try to pass off a piece of ephemera as being older than it actually is. This is not common practice among collectors, but it does happen. These are some of the dates that will help with vintage advertisements:

- Breakfast of Champions (Wheaties, 1935)
- Rush Rush for Orange Crush (1943)
- Finger Lickin' Good (Kentucky Fried Chicken, 1952)
- See the USA in your Chevrolet (1953)
- Look, Ma, no cavities! (Crest, 1958)
- The sign of good bread (Sunblest, 1958)
- Double your pleasure, Double your fun (1959)
- There's always room for Jell-O (1964)
- Have it Your Way (Burger King, 1973)
- Where's the Beef (Wendy's, 1984)

"Good to the Last Drop" is a popular slogan used by Maxwell House Coffee since 1915. It was first used in advertisements by Coca-Cola in 1908.

In 1857, Budweiser adopted the slogan, "King of Bottled Beer." After a few years, it was changed to "King of All Bottled Beers." They continued with that slogan until the introduction of beer cans in 1935. It was then that the slogan was changed to "King of Beers."

The first slogan for Camel cigarettes was "Leave no unpleasant cigaretty after-taste." It was used from 1915 – 1921. At that time, they started using the iconic slogan they would become known for – I'd walk a mile for a Camel."

Coca-Cola advertisements in 1929 showcased their first slogan, "The Pause that Refreshes." In 1932 it was changed to "Ice-cold sunshine." In 1938, they changed their logo to "The best friend thirst ever had." This lasted only a year until it was changed again to "Coca-Cola goes along." The first advertising slogan used by Pepsi was "Twice as Much for a Nickel" in 1939. It was changed to "More Bounce to the Ounce" in 1950.

Tip 48: Following Advertising Mascots 1800's

Advertising Mascots are popular and valuable with collectors. They are known as "cross collectibles" since they are sought after by different types of collectors. For example, the Trix Rabbit would be collected as an animal ephemera and collectors of cereal or advertising mascots. He would also be wanted by rabbit collectors. Many of the mascots fall under the category of cross collectible. Advertising icons of the 1800s include the Michelin Man.

Quaker Oats started using the Quaker Man in their advertisements in 1877. He was the first advertising mascot. His image has changed slightly through the years, but the character is still in use. The Michelin man was introduced in 1898. His appearance has also gone through changes.

Aunt Jemima debuted in 1899. The image was modeled after Nancy Green, a former slave from Kentucky. She toured the country advertising the pancake mix until she passed away in 1923. In 1968 they replaced her bandana with a headband. In 1989, her headband was removed. She was also given earrings and a pearl necklace. Her appearance will give you the age of the advertisements in your collection

Rastus is the cook in the Cream of Wheat advertisements. It first appeared in 1890 and was used until 2020. Frank White, a chef from Chicago, was paid $5 to pose for the photograph.

Tip 49: Timeline of Advertising Mascots 1900s

When searching for vintage advertising ephemera, these are popular mascots and the dates they were introduced:

- Campbell's Kids - Campbell's Soup (1904)
- Morton Salt Umbrella Girl - Morton Salt Company (1914)
- Sailor Jack – Cracker Jacks (1916)
- Gerber Baby – Gerber Baby Food (1928)
- Weinermobile - Oscar Mayer (1936)
- Lil' Squirt – Squirt Soft Drink (1938)
- Popsicle Pete – Popsicle (1939)
- Rosie the Riveter – Westinghouse Electric (1942)
- Miss Chiquita – Chiquita Bananas (1944)
- Captain Morgan – Captain Morgan Rum Company (1944)
- Speedy – Alka Seltzer (1951)
- Catalina – Chicken of the Sea (1952)
- Marky Maypo – Maypo Oatmeal (1956)
- Mr. Clean – Proctor & Gamble (1957)
- Punchy - Hawaiian Punch guy (1961)
- Whipple – Charmin (1965)
- Pillsbury Doughboy – Pillsbury Company (1965)
- Madge – Palmolive (1966)
- Frito Bandito – Fritos (1967)
- Keebler Elves – Keebler Company (1969)
- Twinkie the Kid – Hostess Brands (1971)

Sun-Maid Raisins created the Sun-Maid Girl in May 1915. She was modeled after a painting of Lorraine Collett Petersen. The red bonnet she is wearing is now on display at the Smithsonian. Mr. Peanut was created in 1916 when 14-year-old Antonio Gentile designed him in response to a contest by Planters to create a new icon. Gentile won $5 for his Mr. Peanut drawing. Amedeo Obici, the founder of Planters, later paid for Gentile and his four siblings to go to college.

The Jolly Green Giant was introduced in 1928 as the Jolly Giant. You can tell the age of the Green Giant by his look, which endured a number of changes. In his original look, his skin was white, and he was holding peas. They made him all green in 1930. The word "Jolly" was added to his name in 1935. A year later, they made him taller, had him standing upright, and he was now holding corn. In 1945 he was holding peas and corn. In 1948, he was no longer holding vegetables and was an extremely light shade of green. They had him holding peas again in 1950 and then switched back to him holding corn in 1955. After 1980, they no longer had him holding vegetables. In 1980, he was wearing a red scarf.

Tip 50: Animals in Vintage Advertising Ephemera

Elsie the Cow is one of the most famous animal mascots in the history of advertising. She was introduced in 1936 as the mascot for Borden cheese. Today she has collected keys to 600 cities, led the Rose Bowl parade, and appeared on the cover of cookbooks. In 2000 she was named "one of the top 10 advertising icons of the 20th century." Designers gave Elsie her own family in commercials which included her husband, Elmer. In 1947, when the Borden company invented their bottled glue, they named it after Elmer and used his image in their ads. This is how Elmer's glue was named. These animals can also be found in advertising ephemera:

- Geoffrey the Giraffe – Toys R Us (1948)
- Hamm's Bear – Hamm's Beer (1952)
- Farfel the Dog – Nestle Quick (1953)
- Bucky Beaver – Ipana Toothpaste (1957)
- Charlie the Tuna- Starkist (1961)
- Yipes – Fruit Stripe Gum (1962)
- Axelrod the Dog – Flying A - (1965)
- Woodsy the Owl – United States Forest Service (1970)
- Quicky - Nestle Quick (1973)
- Kool-Aid Man – Kool Aid (1975)

- Spuds MacKenzie – Bud Light Beer (1987)
- Joe Camel – Camel Cigarettes (1988)

The U.S. Forest Service and the Ad Council launched their Smokey Bear advertisements on August 9, 1944, to educate people on how they "can prevent forest fires."

Fresh Up Freddie was a rooster created by Disney in 1957 to advertise 7 Up soft drinks.

Morris the Cat made his debut for 9 Lives in 1968. Bob Martwick rescued Morris from the Humane Society of Hinsdale, Illinois.

Cheetos Mouse advertised Cheetos from 1971 until 1979. Chester Cheetah debuted as the company's new mascot in 1986.

The Pink Drumming Bunny was used from 1973 – 1987 in Duracell Advertisements. In 1988, when their trademark lapsed, Energizer took over the design. They made small changes, including having the bunny wearing his famous black sunglasses and holding the drum sideways instead of lying flat in front of him.

Tip 51: Differences Between Paper Money and Silver Certificates

Silver certificates were produced from 1878-1964 so that people could invest in silver without the need for coins or silver bricks. In addition, they were used to represent the ownership of silver without the need for physical possession. The $1 silver certificate was introduced in 1878 and featured Martha Washington. It was discontinued in 1957. The most collectible silver certificates are 1928C, 1928D, and 1928E. Today the silver certificates cannot be exchanged for silver and are worth slightly more than their face value.

Gold certificates were issued in the same fashion. They showed the worth of gold that the owner invested in. The US seal was a gold color, and the back of the gold certificate was bright orange. Gold certificates were printed from 1865 to 1933. President Franklin Roosevelt announced in 1933 that America was going off the gold standard and ordered that all gold certificates be cashed in by June 5th. However, not all were turned in, so there are a small number of gold certificates available. Because of their rarity, they are higher in value than silver certificates.

Tip 52: Puzzle Makers Through the Years

The first manufacturers of jigsaw puzzles were Ravensburger and Parker Brothers. The puzzles made by Ravensburger were the first to make a soft clicking sound when joined together. As puzzles were made through the years, they took steps to make them trickier by making them in solid colors, in 3-D sizes, and some with images on both sides. Through the years, they also made them with more pieces. As a result, some of the puzzles go up to 26,000 pieces.

In 1931, Frank Ware and John Henriques started making their PAR puzzles after losing their jobs during the Great Depression. The details of their puzzles that stood out were the elevated forms, dropouts within the jigsaw puzzle, and irregular edges. The original logo for the company was the swastika, a Hindu symbol. However, after Hitler adopted the symbol as an image of his hate, they changed it to a seahorse.

In 1974, Steve Richardson and Dave Tibbetts created their line of Stave Puzzles. Their company name is a combination of their first names. These were the first wooden puzzles. Their puzzles are highly sought after by collectors. Smithsonian magazine named them "the Rolls-Royce of jigsaw puzzles."

The company Wrebbit made the first 3D puzzle in 1991. Their line of puzzles was named Puzz-3D. Other puzzle makers include Buffalo Games, Caeco, Sunsout, Liberty Puzzles, Vermont Christmas Company, The New York Puzzle Company, and NAPCO, inc.

Tip 53: History of Restaurant Ephemera

Restaurant ephemera include napkins, sugar packets, advertisements, signs, bags, cartons, and paper cups. The most common of these are menus. Sugar packets were invented in 1944 by Benjamin Eisenstadt.

Colonel Sanders used his own image to advertise his restaurant in 1952, making himself the first restaurant mascot. These restaurants also had mascots that were used in their advertisements and often appeared in person at events:

- Big Boy (Bog Boy's Restaurant) 1936
- Spee-dee (McDonald's) 1948
- Jack (Jack-in-the-Box) 1951
- The King (Burger King) 1955
- Ronald McDonald (McDonald's) 1963
- Wendy (Wendy's Restaurant) 1969
- The Bee (Jollibee) 1980
- Clara Peller - Where's the Beef? (Wendy's) 1984
- The Noid – Domino's Pizza (1986)

Monsieur Boulanger coined the word "restaurant" when he opened the first restaurant in 1765 that he named La Grande Taverne de Londres. When he started, he had one dish to serve, "sheep's feet simmered in white sauce." After that, he added more soups and broths to his line of dishes. Antoine Beauvilliers opened the first modern restaurant in 1782. His restaurant, La Grande Taverne de Londres, was open until 1825. However, it was Escoffier that invented the menu in the 1700s. Delmonico's in New York was the first restaurant in America to have menus for its customers. The restaurant is still open today and continues to serve some of the dishes offered on its first menu. In 1859, the Metropolitan Hotel had the first menu that offered meats cooked in various stages – cold, broiled, fried, or stewed.

Before the early 1900s, children were rarely taken to restaurants. When Prohibition started, restaurants needed to make changes to their meals to make up for the lost revenue from alcohol sales. The Waldorf Astoria led the way in 1921 by creating the first children's menu that included items such as lamb chops and prune whip. The 1900s restaurants had a "women's menu." These menus did not include a price since men were deemed to pay for their meals. Some restaurants still offer these menus, but they are now called "blind menus," and they now give the menu with the prices to the customer who made the reservation. It is no longer based on gender. Other types of menus to build your collection are airline menus, cafeteria menus, catering menus, hospital menus, hotel menus, fast food menus, ships' menus, and railway menus.

Tip 54: Important Comic Book Dates

The first comic book, The Yellow Kid in McFadden's Flats, was published in 1897 by Edward Waterman Townsend. The first superhero was the Phantom, also known as "The Ghost Who Walks." He was introduced on Feb 17, 1936, and first appeared in a comic strip by Lee Falk.

Superman was created by Jerry Siegel and Joe Shuster, high school friends from Cleveland's Glenville High School. They received the copyright for Superman on April 18, 1938. The first Superman comic was sold in June 1938. Batman first appeared in Detective Comics #27 a year later, on May 2, 1939.

There are different stages in the history of comic books. The release of Superman started the Golden Age of Comic Books that ran from 1938-1956. The Silver Age of Comics runs from 1956-1969. The Bronze Age of Comics is the years 1970-1985. The final stage (so far) is the Modern Age of Comic, which runs from 1986 to today.

Tip 55: Notable Creators of Comic Books

Knowing the release of comics will show ephemera collectors where they can begin with their comic book ephemera. This includes the history of the many publishing companies that created superhero comic books. It all started with David McKay Publications in 1882.

Malcolm Wheeler-Nicholson founded National Allied Publications in 1935. Their first comic book was New Fun. This was the first comic written with first-hand material and not based on characters from a comic strip. In 1937, Wheeler-Nicholson teamed with Liebowitz to start Detective Comics, Inc. Wheeler-Nicholson was forced out of his company a year later. The company also became known as DC Comics, although the name was not officially changed until 1977.

Timely Comics was released in 1939 by Martin Goodman. The name was changed to Atlas Comics in 1951 and changed once more in 1961 to Marvel Comics. The Incredible Hulk #1 was published by Marvel on May 10, 1962. These are some of the early characters introduced by Marvel:

- Ka-Zar (1936)
- Human Torch (1939)
- Captain America (1941)
- Hercules (1952)
- Spider-Man (1962)
- Thor (1962)
- Hank Pym (1962)
- Doctor Doom (1962)
- Iceman (1963)
- Doctor Strange (1963)
- Iron Man (1963)
- Professor X (1963)
- Cyclops (1963)
- Hawkeye (1964)
- Black Panther (1966)
- Silver Surfer (1968)
- Falcon (1969)

Marvel and DC Comics are now known as the biggest names in comic books. Early publishing companies of superhero comics include Centaur Publications (1938-1942), Novelty Press (1940-1949), Holyoke Publishing (1941-1946), and AC Comics (1969).

Tower Comics was published between 1965-1969 and brought us T.H.U.N.D.E.R. Agents. Columbia Comics Corporation published Big Shot Comics from May 1940 to August 1949.

Magazine Production published comic books from 1943-1958. They are most known for introducing the Cave Girl and Ghost Rider.

Entertaining Comics (EC Comics) printed a variety of comics from 1944-1956, including children's comics, military, and crime fiction. They are most known for the Tales from the Crypt series.

1First Comics was founded in 1983 by Ken Levin and Mike Gold. They closed in 1991 and relaunched as "First Comics" in 2011.

Tip 56: Comics – Romance, Mysteries, and Westerns

Not all comic books were filled with superheroes. Instead, some told stories behind everyday characters. There were also mysteries, horror, westerns, romance, adventures, humor, and even animals. The first of this type was Sheena, Queen of the Jungle, which was introduced in 1938. The Sheena comic was an imprint by Novelty Press. There were a number of these comic books of these genres published through the years:

- Dell Comics (1929-1974)
- Quality Comics (1937-1956)
- Fiction House (1938-1954)
- Archie Comics (1939)
- Elliot Publishing (1940-1945)
- Novelty Press (1940-1949)
- Harvey Comics (1941-2002)
- Orbit Comics (1945-1955)
- John Publications (1947-1948)
- Star Publications (1949-1954)
- Toby Press (1949-1955)
- Youthful (1949-1954)

- Gold Key Comics (1962-1984)
- Eerie Publications (1966-1981)
- Stanley Publications (1966-1971)
- Skywald Publications (1970-1975)
- Hell Comics (1971-1972)
- Spire Christian Comics (1972-1988)
- Starblaze Graphics (1978-1989)

Crestwood Publications printed Prize Comics, a line that included "Black Magic," a horror comic that ran from 1940-1968. They also produced the "Young Romance" comic from 1947-1963 and the superhero comic, Fighting American from 1954-1989.

T.W.O. Charles Company launched in 1940. Their name was changed to Charlton Comics in 1945. Comic Media started publishing comics in 1952. Their most popular character was Johnny Dynamite. Charlton Comics bought them in 1954.

Tip 57: Comic Strips Through History

Comic Strips and comic books/strips are other popular cross-collected items. Many collectors collect the comics themselves, or they are collectors of the characters in the comic books/strips.

The comic strip was first created by Rodolphe Töpffer in 1837. He was a teacher in France and created comic strips to educate his students. Before Barbie was a fashion doll, she was featured in a comic strip under the name Bild Lilli, a creation of Reinhard Beuthien's for the German newspaper Bild. She was introduced on August 12, 1955. The comic ran until August 12, 1955. The first comic strip in America was the Katzenjammer Kids. Rudolph Dirks created it in 1897.

The Peanuts comic strip was launched on October 2, 1950. Charlie Brown was added on December 21, 1950. Each decade ushered in new comic strips. They are still popular among collectors today:

- The Yellow Kid (1895)

- Mutt and Jeff (November 15, 1907)
- Krazy Kat (October 28, 1913)
- The Gumps (February 12, 1917)
- Gasoline Alley (November 24, 1918)
- Fritzie Ritz (October 9, 1922)
- Moon Mullins (June 19, 1923)
- Little Orphan Annie (August 5, 1924)
- Popeye (January 17, 1929)
- Blondie (September 8, 1930)
- Dick Tracy (October 4, 1931)
- Li'l Abner (August 1934)
- Nancy (October 3, 1938)
- Brenda Starr, Reporter (June 13, 1940)
- Archie (November 1, 1941)
- Gordo (November 24, 1941)
- Hazel (February 13, 1943)
- Rip Kirby (March 4, 1946)
- Pogo (October 4, 1948)
- Beetle Bailey (September 4, 1950)
- Dennis the Menace (March 1951)
- Marmaduke (1954)
- Family Circus (February 29, 1960)
- Doonesbury (October 26, 1970)
- Hägar the Horrible (February 1973)
- Heathcliff (September 3, 1973)
- Cathy (November 22, 1976)
- Garfield (June 19, 1978)
- The Far Side (January 1, 1980)
- Bloom County (December 8, 1980)
- Mother Goose and Grimm (October 1, 1984)
- Calvin & Hobbes (November 18, 1985)
- Dilbert (April 16, 1989)

Tip 58: Magazine Moments to Identify and Collect

Magazines have an interesting history; when you collect them, it is good to know these dates.

The first Playboy magazine did not have a date on it because he did not know if he would make enough money from selling the first magazine to print a second one.

The Scots Magazine was first released in 1739. It is still published today, making it the oldest magazine still in print.

Cosmopolitan magazine went through several changes. When it debuted in 1886, it was a family magazine titled The Cosmopolitan. It later became a literary magazine. Finally, in 1965, it became a women's magazine.

Good Housekeeping was first published on May 2, 1885. It was a black & white publication with no photo on the cover. The issue included several poems, an article about tea and teacups, and Easter customs.

When Fortune magazine started printing in 1929, it was dedicated to photojournalism. However, due to the rising price of ink, it was redesigned as a business magazine in 1948.

Glamour magazine was first published in 1939 under the name Glamour of Hollywood. It was shortened to Glamour in 1943.

When Seventeen magazine debuted in 1944, it was the first magazine for teens.

The first TV Guide was released on April 3, 1953. The photo on the first cover was baby Desiderio Alberto Arnaz IV with Lucille Ball in the corner.

Rolling Stone magazine debuted in 1967. Jann Wenner borrowed from his girlfriend's parents to publish the first issue.

Tip 59: Cereal Ephemera and Their Name Changes

Some cereals changed their names through the years, so you can age your ephemera simply by recognizing the names. One of the earliest breakfast cereals was Pettijohn's Breakfast Food. It was introduced in 1889 by the American Cereal Co. It was sold to the Quaker Oats Company in 1893. They renamed the cereal "Pettijohn's Whole Wheat Cereal" in 1920. Corn Flakes debuted in 1898 as "Sanitas Toasted Corn Flakes." It was changed to Corn Flakes in 1906.

Another cereal with a name change is Ranger Joe Rice Honnies. It was introduced in 1939. When Nabisco bought the cereal in 1954, they changed the name to Rice Honies. The cereal, CheeriOats, was introduced in 1941. They changed their name to Cheerios in 1945. Finally, Freakie Flakes was sold in 1972. A year later, the name was changed to Freakies.

Corn Pops was introduced in 1950. The name went through several changes through the years. They changed their name to Sugar Corn Pops in 1952. It was in 1978 when they removed the word "Corn," naming it "Sugar Pops." In 1984, they decided to remove the word "sugar" and named it Corn Pops. In January 2006, it was named "Pops." This only lasted a few months. Since consumers were against the name change, they went back to using Corn Pops.

A lot of name changes occurred when cereal companies removed the word "Sugar." In 1952, the cereal "Sugar Frosted Flakes" was introduced. In 1983, they changed their name to "Frosted Flakes." Sugar Corn Pops was first sold in 1978. Their name was changed to "Corn Pops" in 1984. Sugar Smacks cereal went through several name changes. First, they were introduced in 1954. Then, they changed their name to Honey Smacks in 1980. Kellogg's changed the name again to "Smacks" in 1992. Finally, in 2004, it was changed back to Honey Smacks.

Tip 60: The Cereal Mascot Timeline

Another beloved part of cereal ephemera is those adorable mascots. They can be found in all three forms – advertisements, signs, and cereal boxes. Again, knowing when the character debuted will help you age your ephemera and not be fooled by a replica. The first character mascot was the Quaker on the Quaker Oats cereal promotions. Sunny Jin followed in 1901; he was the mascot for Force cereal. The gloomy character, Jimmy Dumps, was the creation of Minnie Maud Hanff, who, after eating Force cereal, would transform into Sunny Jin.

- Trix Rabbit (1954)
- Sonny the Cuckoo Bird (Cocoa Puffs) (1962)
- Toucan Sam (1963)
- Sugar Bear (Sugar Crisps) (1965)
- Sir Grapefellow (1972)
- Klondike Pete (Crunchy Nuggets) (1972)
- Buzz Bee (Cheerios) (1979)
- Bid Mixx (1990)

Snap, with Rice Krispies, was introduced in 1932. Crackle and Pop joined him in 1938.

When Kellogg's OKs cereal debuted in 1959, its mascot was Big Otis. In 1961, he was replaced with Yogi Bear.

When Lucky Charms was introduced in 1964, its mascot was Lucky the Leprechaun. He was replaced in 1975 with Waldo, the short red-haired leprechaun.

The first mascot for Cookie Crisp was Cookie Jarvis from 1977 - 1983. In 1981, they introduced Cookie Crook and Cookie Cop (Officer Crumb). In 1990, Chip, the dog.

Sugar Pops cereal debuted in 1951, and its first mascot was Guy Madison, a character from the Adventures of Wild Bill Hickok radio and television show. Sugar Pops sponsored the show, which made Madison the perfect choice. The show ended on September 24, 1958, and their new mascot, Sugar Pops Pete, was introduced in

1959. His character was discontinued in 1967. Their next mascot, Big Yella, was used from 1977-1980.

When Frosted Flakes debuted in 1952, there were four mascots - Tony the Tiger, Newt the Gnu, Elmo the Elephant, and Katy the Kangaroo. They had buyers vote for their favorite, and that character would forever be their chosen mascot. And that is how we got the grrrreat Tony the Tiger!

Sugar Smacks went through several mascots. Knowing when they appeared will tell you how old your ephemera piece is. The cereal was first sold in 1953, and the mascot was Cliffy the Clown. He was discontinued in 1956. Next was Sammy the Seal, who graced Sugar Smacks cereal boxes from 1957 to 1961. Quick Draw McGraw made his appearance in 1961 and was discontinued in 1965. The Smackin' Brothers were the cereal mascots from 1966-1971. They were replaced by a Native American Chief that was used for one year. Finally, dig 'em Frog was introduced. In 1972.

Another cereal company that let the voters choose their favorite mascot was Quaker. In 1965, they introduced two kinds of cereal – Quisp and Quake. Their mascots would even rival each other in commercials. In 1972, they let the children vote on who they liked the most. Quisp won, and so Quake cereal was discontinued. Quake announced his loss in a commercial and introduced his new sidekick, Simon the kangaroo, along with his new cereal, Quangaroos. Once again, in 1979, they let the children vote on which character they liked the best. And once again, Quisp won! Quangaroos cereal was the next to be discontinued.

Tip 61: A History of Playing Cards

No one knows for certain when playing cards were first used. Some believe it was in 1360 in Egypt. Others believe it was that same time period but in China. The earliest written record that mentions playing cards dates back to 1377. It was found in a manuscript written by a German monk named Johannes, who was living in a monastery in Switzerland. He wrote about these "new playing cards" and games that can be played with them. The first decks were hand painted with intricate details.

It was Europeans that first designed the four patterns in cards. They included – coins, swords, cups, and clubs. The early playing cards in Spain had 40 cards in a deck. The number cards only went up to seven. There were no eights, nines, tens, or queens. The card we know as the Jack was called the Prince or the Knave. When the playing cards were taken to Germany, they changed the suits to Hearts, Bells, Acorns, Leaves (Spades). They also added queens and aces to the deck.

More changes came along in the 1400s when France made decks of playing cards in two colors – red and black. They also introduced playing cards in hearts, diamonds, clubs (clovers), and spades (piques). In 1860, card makers in America added the Joker. This card was initially called the "Best Bower." Finally, in 1864, playing card makers changed card designs by adding the value indicators and suits to the corner of the cards. This allowed players to "squeeze" their cards together and still see everything they were holding. These became known as "squeezers."

In 1835, Lewis Cohen invented the machine that printed "all four colors of the card faces at once." In 1871, he opened the New York Consolidated Company. He introduced Bee playing cards in 1892.

Andrew Dougherty started producing Tally-Ho Playing Cards in 1881. That same year, on June 28, 1881, Russel, Morgan & Co also started manufacturing playing cards. The company name was changed to the United States Printing Company in 1885 when they introduced their Bicycle brand playing cards. They changed their name again in 1894 to the United States Playing Card Company.

Types of playing card games that can be included in your ephemera collection are Uno cards, Old Maid, Pinochle, Poker, Pokemon, Magic, Rook, and Skip-Bo. In addition, there are a wide variety of designs found on playing cards today. They include advertisements, historical landmarks, fun facts, recipes, national flags, animals, and automobiles. Also include the round playing cards known as "Round Rondo Playing Cards."

Chapter 5: The Ephemera Community

- Inside the Ephemera Society of America
- What Autograph Collectors Should Know
- Social Media Groups for Collectors
- Clubs for Playing Card Collectors
- Meet Trading Card Collectors

The Importance of Meeting Collectors

One of the biggest joys of collecting ephemera is meeting more ephemera collectors! It is not just for fun, but it is important to meet collectors. They can be your resource for historical information and can also relay information on ways and locations to buy and sell ephemera. There are many ways to meet collectors – social media, clubs, conventions, and trade shows.

Tip 62: The Importance of the Ephemera Society of America

The British Ephemera Society was launched in 1975. The Ephemera Society of America followed the establishment of the group in 1980. They offer a variety of resources that can be found on their website.

Some of the features on their website are online exhibits, a series of blogs, links to ephemera organizations and resourceful websites, and access to past issues of their Ephemera Journal. For members, there is also the monthly newsletter, eNews.

They hold several opportunities for ephemera collectors to meet. Their annual conference is held in Connecticut and includes exhibits that tell stories pertaining to different subjects. Each year, undergraduate and graduate students are invited to give a presentation on how ephemera reflected on their schoolwork. This shows the importance of ephemera in society. Their annual fair is a grand exhibit for ephemera collectors, buyers, and enthusiasts. They also host a "mid-year get-together" every fall. This event is held in different locations across the country.

There are different styles of ephemera shows held across the country throughout the year, and the Ephemera Society has a list of these on its website (www.ephemerasociety.org/events-calendar).

Tip 63: Label Collector Groups

The Labologist Society was launched in England in 1958 by three collectors of beer labels. Today they have several chapters, including America. The full name of their club is the International Society for Beer Label Collectors and Brewery research.

The first orange labels were manufactured in 1885. Nearly 100 years later, in 1981, the Citrus Label Society was founded by Lorne Allmon to celebrate the collecting of citrus labels. Their mission was to create a place for citrus label collectors to meet and share information, trade labels, and citrus-related events. They are located in Southern California and often host events throughout the area. Their website features meeting dates, articles, and the history of citrus labels. When collecting citrus labels, remember that though there have been thousands of designs through the years, the size has remained the same at 10x11 inches.

Tip 64: Facebook Groups for Ephemera Collectors

Facebook is home to the "Bookmark Collectors Club." they explore the history of bookmarks and share photos of their collection. The International Friends of Bookmarks has members from around the world. They were established in 2015. Joe Stephenson launched the Bookmark Society in 1991. They hold swap meets for their members twice a year. The Stevengraph Collectors Association is dedicated to collectors of bookmarks created by Thomas Stevens. These clubs for ephemera collectors can also be found on Facebook:

- Beer-Labels Collectors
- Matchbook Covers
- All Sports Card Collecting
- Circus Poster Collectors
- Ideals Magazine Collecting Group
- Real Autograph Collectors Club
- Collectible Movie Poster Page
- 1890-1930 Sheet Music Collectors
- Vintage Photography Collecting
- Vintage Movie Poster Collectors Club
- Vintage Postcards from the Past
- Vintage Paper and Fruit and Veggie Crate Label Collectors

Tip 65: Ephemera Groups on Social Media

Social Media is filled with collectors around the world. Among the shows on YouTube, there are collectors that educate on a variety of topics related to ephemera. These YouTube shows were made for different ephemera collectors:

- 49dragonflies
- The Paper Outpost
- Tracie for Creative
- Book and Paper Arts

The Scrappy Wife has a series of videos that are dedicated to scrapbooking, but among them are tutorials on storing ephemera that can provide valuable knowledge for collectors.

Kollecting Kaos has a focus on comic books. These educational videos cover the value of a comic, selling and buying, and cleaning comics.

Instagram and Twitter have a large ephemera following. On Instagram, you can find ephemeramagnets, ephemeradinners, pgsnailmailer, and ephemera bazaar. On Twitter, collectors can find

Ephemera Podcast, Wrestling Trading Cards, and Cool Movie Posters.

Pinterest has several boards dedicated to collecting bookmarks. Those pages include "Don't Bend the Page" by Michelle Pietsch, "Bookmark ideas" by Mandy O'Neill, "Bookmarkers" by Anne West, and "Bookmarks – Mark My Place." These Pinterest boards can be a further resource for ephemera collectors.

Tip 66: Using Meetup to Meet Up

You can also meet collectors for buying and selling or just for friendship to share collecting stories through Meetup. People across the country use this app to help you meet people with the same interests in your area.

You can also start your own Meetup group to reach out to neighboring ephemera collectors. You can also use this to arrange your own events for collectors. To do this, go to the website, MeetUp.com and at the top of the page, click on "Start a New Group." From there, follow the steps to organize your group and choose a name for your group; it can always be changed later. It is free to use the website to reach out to others, but there is a monthly fee to start a group.

Tip 67: Blogs for Ephemera Collectors

Collectors find blogs a fun way to communicate with fellow collectors. They are also great places to buy and sell ephemera. These are some of the blogs made as a communication hotspot for ephemera collectors:

- Books and Paper Fairs (old books and ephemera)
- Ephemera Obscura (ephemera variety)
- Remember When Postcards Blog (postcards and trade cards)

- Artifact Collectors (photographs, advertisements, stamps, paper money)

The blogs "Mark My Place," by Debrah Gai Lewis, "Bookmarks Collections from around the World" by Liudmala, and "A World of Bookmarks" are dedicated to the history of bookmarks and sharing photos of bookmarks they collected from many different places. The blog "It's Called Bookmarking" explores how to organize and store bookmarks. Finally, "Forgotten Bookmarks" is a fun blog started by a bookseller who wanted to share the many things he found in books that readers used as bookmarks. These include items such as recipe cards, green stamps, postcards, tickets, and notes.

The blog, Autograph Hound's Blah Blah Blog, is written by Lew (Autograph Hound), who shares her experiences at autograph conventions and resources for fellow collectors. The blog, Author by the Letters, was started by Tom Owens, who started collecting baseball autographs in 1972. His blog chronicles his history of collecting autographs through the mail (TTM).

Tip 68: Rise & Fall of the Comics Magazine Association of America

In 1954, Psychiatrist Fredric Wertham wrote "Seduction of the Innocent," a book filled with allegations that comic books were corrupting children. He claimed that Superman carried fascist values, that Batman and Robin were living a homosexual lifestyle, and that Wonder Woman "was a lesbian with a bondage fixation." The details of his book sent parents into a frenzy. This alarmed Congress, who felt the need to investigate, beginning with calling Wertham to testify before the Senate Subcommittee on Juvenile Delinquency. Comic Book publishers agreed to oversee any dangerous content that could be detrimental to children. To do this, they formed the Comics Magazine Association of America. The group created the Comics Code Authority, a list of regulations for comic book publishers to follow to lessen the concern of comic books being a negative influence. These are some of the changes they agreed to issue:

1. Crimes shall never be presented in such a way as to create sympathy for the criminal, promote distrust of the forces of law and justice, or inspire others with a desire to imitate criminals.
2. Police officers, judges, government officials, and respected institutions shall never be presented in such a way as to create disrespect for established authority.
3. Scenes or instruments associated with the walking dead, torture, vampires and vampirism, ghouls, cannibalism, and werewolfism are prohibited.
4. Respect for parents, the moral code, and for honorable behavior shall be fostered. A sympathetic understanding of the problems of love is not a license for morbid distortion.

Stan Lee was the first to say that these rules were too strict. They agreed. In 1971, they started taking steps to relax their regulations. The first was to say, "Vampires, ghouls, and werewolves shall be permitted to be used when handled in the classic tradition." In the year 2000, publishers started leaving the organization. By 2010, only three publishers were left in the organization – Archie Comics, Bongo Comics, and DC Comics. In 2010, Bongo also left the group. Archie Comics and DC Comics followed in January 2011.

Tip 69: The Antique Advertising Association of America

The Antique Advertising Association of America (AAAA) was founded in 1990. Today it is the largest club dedicated to collecting vintage advertisements. Members receive the Membership Directory Booklet to communicate with each other. The directory includes the contact information of each member and their specific collecting interests. Some members even invite others to their homes to see their collection in person. That information is also included in the directory.

They hold an annual 4-day convention every July. The event includes "room sales" by collectors who display their items in a way that looks like a general store from the 1800s. There is also a silent auction, presentations with guest speakers, games, and the "Favorite Advertising Exhibit."

They print an award-winning quarterly newsletter, PastTimes, which releases news about collecting and club information. During the months that PastTimes is not published, they release an e-newsletter, the Checkerboard. In addition, they feature current events in the collector's world, amazing finds, auction dates, and a wanted section.

Tip 70: Autograph University for Collectors

Autograph University is a prime resource for autograph collectors. Their website is filled with advice on the best ways to obtain and collect autographs. Collectors can access articles and ebooks that offer advice on autograph etiquette, locating autographs, and links to more resources. There are also informative videos that include how to obtain autographs through the mail (TTM) and how to frame autographs to display and preserve them. The group also offers a free template to create an event calendar. Matt Raymond, the man behind the Autograph University, also hosts the web show "Autograph University Master Class."

When you get autographs for photographs, the best marker to use is a blue sharpie. If the photo has a dark background, then use a silver sharpie.

Tip 71: Significance of the Ross Art Group

Mickey Ross established the Ross Art Group in 1994 with his private collection of vintage and original posters that he had saved for over ten years. This is a good place to start if you want to add posters to your ephemera collection (or even your home or office décor). Today, the gallery displays more than 2,500 vintage posters for collectors and enthusiasts to enjoy. Of course, an appointment needs to be made to visit the gallery, and they do their best to accommodate visitors.

Posters can be purchased from the gallery and through their website, postergroup.com. Their posters, which expand 230 years, are all originals. They ship posters internationally for those who cannot visit in person. The group also has framing services available. With over 2,000 frames to choose from, they can encase posters, ephemera, artwork, and any item that you would like to preserve. For those in their neighboring community of Boca, Raton, they offer delivery and installation.

Tip 72: A Society of Playing Card Collectors

The International Playing-Card Society was established in Europe in 1972 for collectors of playing cards and card games. They host an annual event and quarterly meetings in London.

The Playing Card Collectors Club on Facebook is home to over 9,000 collectors of playing cards. They share their findings and compare information to help each other build their collections.

In 1985, the 52 Plus Joker Club was established for playing card collectors. In 1985 they partnered with the Chicago Playing Card Collectors Club, making them the largest playing card society in the world. They also have a YouTube show with a host of videos filled with fun information and interaction for playing card collectors. In addition, they hold an annual convention with guest speakers and a chance to buy cards from vendors (or set up your own table). One attraction at the event is the "Table Spotlight." This gives a collector a chance to stand up and talk about how he started collecting playing cards and interesting sets he found along the way. He can also display cards that he has for sale or trade.

Tip 73: Places to Meet Trading Card Collectors

The Trade Cardz Zone, Trading Card Central, and CardzReview are forums for collectors of all types of trading cards. In addition, there are a number of baseball card forums for collectors to meet, trade information, and buy, sell, and trade their baseball cards. To be safe, ask the collector to send a photo of the baseball card and another one of them holding it. These forums are a good place to find vintage and newer baseball cards.

- Blowout Cards
- Cardboard Connection
- SportsCardForum
- Sports Card Club

Vintage Card Traders was launched on July 23, 1999. They were originally an online group comprised of baseball card collectors over the age of 18 who wanted a safe place to buy, sell, and trade their cards. They have since grown to include collectors of pre-1980 football, hockey, and basketball cards.

Collect-a-Con is the largest trading card show in the United States. The group tours across the country, holding monthly shows with celebrity guest speakers and over 500 vendors. The website, www.collectaconusa.com, has information on dates and scheduled speakers.

Tip 74: Piecing Together Puzzle Collectors

Puzzles were invented in 1760 by a mapmaker named John Spilsbury. He made his first puzzle by gluing a map to a piece of cardboard and cutting it into pieces. He promoted it as a learning tool, hoping to teach geography to children. However, they were first sold to the wealthy because they cost $3-$5, which was a hefty price for working families at that time since they earned $30-$50 a month.

Spilsbury originally named them "dissected maps." The name was changed to "jigsaw puzzle" in 1880. Many people believe it was named after the jigsaw, "the device used to cut the pieces." but it was not. The saw that was first used to cut the pieces was the marquetry saw. The jigsaw was not invented until 1855.

Those who collect puzzles or are just fascinated with building puzzles are called "dissectologists." This is a reflection of the original name of puzzles – dissected maps." William Shortz later coined the word "enigmatology," which is the study of puzzles. To this day, Shortz is the only person to hold a degree in Enigmatology. Today, one of the world's most famous puzzle builders can be found on YouTube. Karen Puzzles (not her real name) has a YouTube show that educates how to work through and build an array of puzzles, including solid colors, 24,000 pieces, and ones with holograph pieces. She has conquered every puzzle sent her way!

PAR puzzles used to include a suggested time on how long it will take to complete a puzzle. This was based on how fast they put the puzzle together. The challenge was called "beat the PAR time." Today puzzle builders see how fast they can build their puzzles as a personal challenge. The World Jigsaw Puzzle Competition is held every year in Spain. The crowning champion is the one who can build their puzzle the fastest.

The Philippines is the home of Georgina Gil-Lacuna, the world's largest puzzle collector, as recognized by the Guinness World Records. Her collection of over 1,500 puzzles can be seen at the Puzzle Mansion in Tagaytay, Cavite, Philippines. This puzzle museum is also a bed and breakfast!

The Jigsaw Puzzle Swap Exchange is an amazing group of puzzle enthusiasts from the United States, Australia, and Europe who exchange puzzles, so there is always something new to build. The group has over 4,000 puzzles to select from. When they finish building the puzzle, they pass it on to the next person and receive another puzzle to build.

Chapter 6: Collectors Celebrating Ephemera

- Notable Days for Collectors
- Clubs for Postcard Collectors
- Inside Collect-a-Con
- Celebrating the History of Playing Cards
- Museums for Every Collectors Bucket List

Celebrating and Recognizing Collectibles

One of the most exciting parts about collecting ephemera is celebrating your collection with others. Collectors show their joy in collecting through clubs, conventions, and even having a special day that recognizes their collectibles.

Tip 75: Notable Days Celebrated by Ephemera Collectors

World Photo Day is on August 19, and it celebrates the day when the French government purchased the patent for the daguerreotype process. These National Days celebrate different types of ephemera and are often marked with parties, fairs, and conventions:

- National Sticker Day is celebrated on January 13.
- Indian Newspaper Day is celebrated on January 29.
- World Trading Card Day is celebrated on February 24.
- World Bookmark Day is celebrated on February 25.
- Paper Money Day is celebrated on March 10.
- National Greeting Card Day is celebrated on April 1.
- Read a Road Map Day is celebrated on April 5.
- National Scrapbook Day is the first Saturday in May.
- National Magazine Day is celebrated on May 21.
- World Tarot Day is celebrated on May 25.

- National US Postage Stamp Day is celebrated on July 1.
- National Comic Book Day is celebrated on September 25.
- National Newspaper Week – begins on the first Sunday in October
- World Postcard Day is celebrated on October 1.
- National Playing Card Collection Day is celebrated on October 17

Tip 76: Ephemera in the Toy Hall of Fame

The Toy Hall of Fame has added toys that fall under the umbrella of ephemera! The National Toy Hall of Fame at the Strong was established in 1991 to recognize toys that impacted "the world of play and imagination" and maintained a level of popularity. For those who collect all types of ephemera, you can boost your collection by adding pieces that you can boast have found a spot in the Hall of Fame.

The first ephemera toy to enter the Hall of Fame was the jigsaw puzzle in 2002. Puzzles are known to have a positive impact on lives in several ways. Puzzles have become devices used for meditation. They are used as tools to work with autistic children. They help build your memory and concentration, which is good exercise for the brain. They have even helped the memories of patients with Alzheimer's disease. The biggest role of the puzzle is a toy!

In 2005, the Cardboard Box became the next ephemera product to earn a place in the Toy Hall of Fame. It was England that created the first cardboard box. But, the children recognized the cardboard box as a toy. With their creativity, they made endless toys, including cars, houses, spaceships, kitchen appliances, castles, and TVs for the larger boxes. Shoe boxes were transformed into garages for toy cars, boats, airplanes, and dollhouses. Even smaller boxes were crafted into cars and dollhouse furniture.

Playing cards were added in 2010. Seven years later, the paper airplane was inducted. In 2018, the Uno cards were added, and a year later, the Magic Cards joined the Toy Hall of Fame. The coloring book also joined the Magic Cards in 2019.

Tip 77: Clubs for Ephemera Collectors

The Grolier Club was established in 1884 and still going strong! The club members are collectors of books and graphic art on paper.

A group of poster stamp collectors met in 2004 to form the Poster Stamp Collectors Club. They aim to serve as an educational beacon for enthusiasts and a place for collectors to meet.

The American Historical Print Collectors Society was founded in 1975 for collectors of American photographs at least 100 years old.

The Universal Autograph Collectors Club offers autographs for purchase, the Pen & Quill magazine, and a directory of autograph dealers.

The Original Paper Doll Artists Guild was established in 1984 for collectors and paper doll artists. The group holds an annual convention and offers a quarterly newsletter that covers their annual convention, tips for artists, and historical information.

Tip 78: Clubs to Meet Postcard Collectors

The Taconic Postcard Club was established in 2002. They hold monthly meetings at the Yorktown Museum in the Yorktown Community and Cultural Center.

The Lancaster County Postcard Club is a Facebook group for postcard collectors to meet and share information. They hold monthly meetings at the Farm and Home Center in Lancaster.

The Denver Postcard Club is dedicated to preserving and sharing postcard history. Their monthly meetings are free and open to the public. The group reaches out to share their love of collecting with children at Children's Hospital Colorado. Twice a year, they send packets of postcards and stamps to the hospital accompanied with a list of ways to teach and enjoy postcard collecting with the children. They donate postcards that date back to 1930 to the Denver Library's Western History Collection. When they receive letters and postcards written by military personnel from World War II, they donate them to the Legacy Project.

The Washington Crossing Card Collectors Club includes members from eastern Pennsylvania and New Jersey. There are many events for members to attend, including an annual picnic, annual dinner, and monthly meetings that include an auction and door prizes. In addition, there are monthly newsletters, discounts on postcard collecting supplies and books, and access to books and periodicals related to the history of postcards.

The Metropolitan Postcard Club of New York City was founded in 1946 and is now the oldest postcard club in the United States. Members include dealers and collectors from around the world to share information and buy, sell, and trade postcards. Monthly meetings are free for members and $3 for collectors and enthusiasts who have not yet joined.

Tip 79: Clubs and Events for Business Card Collectors

American Business Card Club was established in 1980 and now has members from around the world who routinely trade business cards through the mail. The monthly newsletter, CARD TALK, is filled with information about everything business cards.

Business cards can be saved in file boxes and plastic storage card cases. There are also business card books of different sizes. There are sheet protectors sized for business cards that can be saved in a 3-ring binder.

Tip 80: Paper Money Collector Clubs

The WORLD PAPER MONEY Collectors Club is a Facebook group of over 17,000 members. They share historical information, help collectors find the value of their paper money, and serve as a place to buy and sell their paper money.

Banknoteclub.com is a meeting place for paper money collectors from all over. They describe how paper money enthusiasts describe banknotes as "an endless trip through different cultures, societies, areas of knowledge, art and more." For collectors in America and various other countries, their website includes contact information for the dealers and their areas of interest and expertise.

The San Diego Paper Money Club was established for collectors of paper money from around the world. They hold monthly meetings that focus on different topics each month. They also invite collectors to bring in their favorite pieces to show. Their website serves as a database that includes links to resources for studying the history of paper money.

The Society of Paper Money Collectors was organized to "promote the study and appreciation of paper money and related financial history." Club members have access to several benefits. Their website lists information on upcoming shows and events, links to social media pages for paper money collectors, and a directory of dealers in the United States and the United Kingdom. Members also receive a bi-monthly journal and access to their past issues for research. The Society also has a variety of awards that are gifted throughout the year.

Tip 81: Events and Clubs for Matchbook Collectors

In September 1892, Joshua Pusey developed the concept of holding paper matches in a "book." He wanted something more convenient to carry matches in so people would not have to carry matchboxes. He called his creation the "flexible match." With his design, they opened and closed in a similar way to a book. Later that month, Charles Bowman of Philadelphia developed the modern matchbook cover. The Binghamton Match Company manufactured the first matchbooks in 1893. Diamond Match Company sued them because they bought the copyright from Pusey for $4,000. They released their matchbooks a year later. Kaeser & Blair released their matchbooks in 1895. Matchbooks that are most collectible are the extra-long matchbooks made before 1883 and matchbooks made between 1894 and 1929.

Henry Traute was a salesman for Diamond, and in 1902 he set out to promote matchbooks as advertising material, calling them "mini billboards." The first company to advertise on matchbooks was Pabst Brewing Company. It was also Traute's suggestion to write "Close Cover Before Striking" on the matchbook covers.

Matchbook covers can be stored in plastic sheet protectors and kept in a 3-ring binder. They can be organized in several ways, from newest to oldest, in groups by company name or state. Some are also stored by categories such as banks, garages, gas stations, and hotels. Choose a category or pattern that works best for your collection. When you store your matchbooks, first remove the matches and then flatten the covers. The only time collectors do not remove the matches is when there is artwork on the matches, called "features," or words written on them called "printed sticks. When matches are kept intact, they are called "full-books."

The Rathkamp Matchcover Society is the largest and oldest club for matchbook collectors. They hold an annual banquet, and each year they reward a club member who sponsors the most new members. California matchbook clubs are the Angelus Matchcover Club and Sierra-Diablo Matchcover Club.

Tip 82: Explore the Annual Metro Vintage Advertising Collectors Show

In 1998, Retro Petro held the first Metro Vintage Advertising Collectors Show under the name "Metro Petro." The show was held at the Old Feed Mill Auction in Boonton, New Jersey, for collectors and enthusiasts of automobile and vintage advertisements, garage art, and petroliana. Today, with their new name, the "Annual Metro Vintage Advertising Collectors Show," their event is held in Pompton, New Jersey, and includes free parking and free admission. Along with buying and selling vintage ads, guests can enter for door prizes and receive a complimentary copy of their Automobilia magazine.

Tip 83: Inside the Original Paper Doll Artists Guild

The Original Paper Doll Artists Guild was founded in 1984 to promote and support collecting paper dolls. Their quarterly magazine, Paper Doll Studio, includes historical information and artwork of paper dolls designed by artists and fashion designers. Their website includes an informative blog, tips on drawing paper dolls, a history of the dolls, instructions on preservation, advice on collecting, and even a free paper doll! Their website is the epicenter for paper doll information.

One of the club's highlights is their 5-day Annual Paper Doll Convention which falls under a fun theme. Some of the last few themes were "Tell Me a Story," "Mystery, Murder & Mayhem," "Entertainment Extravaganza," and "The 1960s." There are three ways to attend the show. The full Convention Registration includes the souvenirs and the Guest Registration with no souvenirs. They also have an Absentee Registration for those who would like to collect the souvenirs but cannot attend the show. Among the souvenirs are three dinners and an invitation to the reception party. Expand your ephemera collection with paper doll souvenir books and programs. There is also a wide assortment of exhibits and displays, workshops, and competitions at the show. There is a raffle room, a sales room, and even a freebie table.

Tip 84: Groups and Events Just for Comic Collectors

Every Labor Day in Georgia, collectors and enthusiasts enjoy the annual Dragon Con. This annual event started in 1987 and celebrates "science fiction & fantasy, gaming, comics, literature, art, music, and film." Ephemera collectors will find a vast amount of paper items for their collection at Dragon Con.

Houston hosts Comicpalooza, an annual event dedicated to comics and related items. A Literature Conference, Cultural Arts Avenue, exciting exhibits, and live podcasts are inside the convention. Their website, Comicpalooza.com, is filled with convention information for collectors.

MegaCon is one of the largest events in America dedicated to comics, science fiction, horror, anime, and gaming. Orlando is home to the 4-day event. Information about their upcoming conventions can be found on their website, Megacon.com.

Comic-Con is the crown jewel of events for comic collectors. It all started in March 1970 as a one-day event at the US Grant Hotel in San Diego and was originally called the San Diego West Coast Comic Convention. They had great success, so they held another show in August, which was a 3-day event this time. The name was changed to Comic-Con in 1973. The tradition of coming dressed as your favorite characters started in 1974. Today Comic-Cons are 4-day events. Each Comic-Con has a program for those attending. These are sought after by ephemera collectors. When searching for vintage programs, remember Jack Kirby designed the cover of the first program.

Tip 85: Celebrating Circus Ephemera

Circus World is a historical site dedicated to the history of the circus. The site is located in Baraboo, Wisconsin, home of the Ringling Brothers. The site includes seven large buildings filled with circus memorabilia.

The Circus Fans Association was launched in 1929 with the purpose of preserving the history of the American circus. They were the first society of this kind. They provide educational resources on the history of the circus and an opportunity to meet and communicate with fellow circus enthusiasts and collectors. Their bi-monthly magazine, White Tops, was first published in May 1927. Today it can be read on their website.

The Circus Historical Society was established in 1939, and today the group includes historians, writers & researchers, educators, collectors, circus staff members, and people who just adore everything about the circus. They publish the quarterly journal, Bandwagon. They have back issues on their website: circushistory.org/about-bandwagon. They run the message board, Jackpot Journal, for collectors and enthusiasts to share stories. Circus ephemera is passed out at the annual convention, making a great addition to your collection.

Tip 86: Fairs and Events for Ephemera Collectors

The International Money Fair includes dealers, investors, and collectors from around the world. In addition, the show includes an auction and exhibitors of paper money, bonds, and shares.

The New York Antiquarian Book Fair has over 200 vendors with a wide amount of ephemera that are not sold at a high cost. The ephemera available included incunabulum, manuscripts, maps, illustrations, historical documents, and prints. The subjects of the ephemera are science, art, medicine, history, fashion, religion, and politics.

Papermania Plus has been an annual event in Hartford, Connecticut, since 1975. There is an incredible number of ephemera at this paper show. The exhibits were divided into categories:

1. Memorabilia and Keepsakes: Autographs, Personal Letters, Photography, Valentines, and Greeting cards, Stamps
2. Pop Culture: Prints, Posters, Magazines, Advertisements, Flyers, Sports, Movies, and Comic Books

3. Posters and Postcards: The postcards are cataloged by city and state.
4. Books and Ephemera: Menus, Theater Programs, Catalogs, Political Stickers, Maps, Documents, Trade cards, Sheet Music, Baseball cards, and Concert Tickets

Tip 87: Museums Dedicated to Ephemera

Lilek's Matchbook Museum is an online museum for matchbook collectors that includes images and history behind the matchbooks on display.

Photo Antiquities Museum of Photographic History in Pittsburgh, Pennsylvania, opened its doors in 1993. The museum includes a collection of over 2,000 cameras. Their collection of over 500,000 photographs includes Daguerreotypes, Ambrotypes, Tintypes, Lantern Slides, Stereo Views, and paper processes.

There are museums across the country that celebrate and preserve the history of ephemera. For example, the Ringling Circus Museum opened its doors in 1948. Circus ephemera inside the museum include posters, handbills, art prints, circus records, literature, photos, and even newspaper clippings that date back to 1816.

The Poster House was the first poster museum in America. The plans for the museum began in 2015 and opened to the public on June 20, 2019. Their goal is to "present the impact, culture, and design of posters, both as historical documents and methods of contemporary visual communication."

The Milner Library at Illinois State University holds the Circus and Allied Arts Collection. It includes programs, route books, art books, photographs, business records, and posters. At the Princeton University Library, collectors can enjoy circus documents, photographs, letters, and scrapbooks.

The Chicago Postcard Museum celebrates the history of Chicago through picturesque postcards. This is a virtual museum, so it can be viewed from around the world. They show the front and back of all of the postcards.

The National Museum of the Playing Card is in Turnhout, Belgium. They house a history of playing cards that dates back 400 years. It includes an exhibit titled "5 of Hearts" that details violent outcomes from card games, how the church attempted a role in playing cards, the political impact of playing cards, and how fortune tellers used playing cards through the years.

Chapter 7: Care Rules for Ephemera Collectors

- What to Avoid Doing When Collecting Ephemera
- What Collectors Need to Store Stamps Safely
- Safe Ways to Clean Ephemera
- Insuring Your Ephemera Collection
- Storing and Preserving Large Ephemera

Protecting, Preserving, and Displaying Your Ephemera

As fun as it is to search for ephemera and watch your collection grow, it is equally important to handle and protect your ephemera. There are some cleaning tips that collectors can handle, but for large repairs – and always when in doubt – contact a professional. By following these guidelines, your ephemera will last for years to enjoy.

Tip 88: What NOT to Do When Collecting Ephemera

Do not store your ephemera in an area where it is in direct contact with sunlight for longer than an hour.

Do not use any erasers to clean paper money. And do not use an iron to flatten the bills.

Do not store ephemera in rooms that are too hot. The ideal temperature is 65°F and 72°F.

Do not place your collection on the floor. Any type of flooding can cause permanent damage.

Do not store ephemera in cardboard boxes. That puts them at risk of pests or insects.

Do not store stamps in plastic bags or loosely in a box. They can stick to each other and get scratched, torn, or wrinkled.

Do not clean baseball cards, not even swiping the top. Baseball cards should only be cleaned by professionals.

Do not store ephemera in the attic, basement, or garage, even if they are in storage boxes. These are places of high humidity that will cause mold to grow.

Do not place any type of damp items on top of your collection, even if the paper is safely stored in boxes. Your collection needs to have air circulating around the items.

Do not allow food and beverages around your collection. Spills can happen easily, and damage lasts forever. If you just ate, wash your hands before you handle the ephemera pieces.

Tip 89: Proper Ways to Display Ephemera

If you want to hang old photographs, attach a piece of plastic to the back. This creates a vapor lock and prevents them from molding.

If you want to display your paper collectibles, putting them in frames behind glass or plexiglass is the safest way to do that. Be sure to use a mat inside the frame. This allows an air pocket for the paper to breathe. The mat should be made of acid-free paper. Use frames that have a glass covering with UV protection.

When storing or displaying autographs in frames, keep them upright, so the ink does not run, and always use the acid-free mat on the back to keep the signature from touching the glass and smudging.

Tip 90: Do This First to Store Ephemera

If the documents have been folded, open them up and store them completely flat. Those creases will disintegrate the paper over time, causing them to tear.

Avoid rolling up maps and posters when storing them. Instead, place them in polyester bags and lay them flat. There are hanging file folders large enough to store them.

Newspaper clippings should be stored flat and away from other paper. The ink from the newspaper can stain other types of ephemera. Make a photocopy of them to have a record of the content in the articles and advertisements.

Tip 91: How to Store Your Collection

Acid-free products will protect your ephemera from damage and aging. Sheet protectors, boxes, and filing folders can all be bought in acid-free options. If you use zip-style bags to store your ephemera, include a sheet of acid-free paper for protection. Archival boxes and envelopes (Mylar or Melinex) are the best to use because archival products are resistant to the elements that cause the paper to deteriorate. Items that are lignin-free are safe for your ephemera. Lignin is an acid that can damage paper.

Craft stores sell cases for storing photographs that are great for storing ephemera. If you do not have much storage space, use plastic envelopes for storing CDs and DVDs. These will allow you to store more ephemera in a smaller box. In addition, you can add a piece of Velcro to close the plastic envelopes securely. These are especially beneficial when storing them because they are the same size and shape.

Some of the agents that can damage ephemera are light, moisture, dust, pollution, insects, rodents, and time. Ephemera should be preserved and displayed in a cool, dry environment and away from direct sunlight. Make sure to maintain a steady temperature. If the temperature fluctuates, it can cause the paper to deteriorate quicker.

Use plastic sleeves from photo albums or archival envelopes to store smaller pieces of ephemera. Stock sheets and album pages come in several sizes and can fit recipe cards, matchbooks, business cards, paper money, checks, tickets, bank notes, documents, photographs, and postcards. When using album pages, add corner mounts to hold the ephemera safely. You can also use sheet protectors designed for baseball cards and save them in a 3-ring binder. File folders can hold ephemera and can be stored in a filing cabinet. Hanging files would be best there.

For storing catalogs, chapbooks, and magazines, use mylar sleeves. L-Sleeves are the best to use when storing documents and photographs. The static cling keeps the documents in place and closes in a way that does not allow dust to access the papers.

Plastic shoe boxes and aluminum cases can also be used for storing ephemera, as long as the ephemera items inside are also in protective covers. Scrapbooking cases can also be used as storage boxes for different sizes of ephemera. Keep them in an open area such as shelves and bookcases where the air can circulate and prevent mold.

Tip 92: Proper ways to Store and Preserve Stamps

Stamp Albums were introduced in the 1860s. They include outlines that are the same shape as stamps and, in some, the image of the stamp. Stamps are placed inside using strips called "hinges" that were made from glassine. Through time, when the stamps are removed, the hinges leave discolored marks on the back and sometimes cause them to tear. When buying and selling stamps, collectors use the term "Mint Never Hinged (NMH)" to describe vintage stamps that were saved in an album without the use of hinges. Collectors can now purchase mounts to slide their stamps into when using stamp albums, so they no longer need the hinges. That way, the stamps do not receive the damage caused by hinges. Mounts can be bought in the size of the stamps or purchased in strips that can be sized to match the stamps by using a mount cutter. After you adhere the mount to the page, let it dry before adding the stamp.

When selecting an album for storing stamps, use one with a waterproof cover and sheet protectors made with PET material, a lightweight plastic resistant to bacteria. Another album for stamp collectors is Stock Books. Many collectors use these to store their duplicate stamps. These albums have strips that are plastic or glassine. There is also another protective sheet cover between the pages that prevent stamps from being pressed together. Stock sheets can also be bought separately and stored in a traditional 3-ring binder.

Stamps should be stored at least six feet off the floor/ground. Check your stamps on a regular basis for water damage, discoloration, or infestation. If any of this occurs, move it to a new page or cards.

Tip 93: Organizing Your Ephemera Collection

After you decide what items to store your ephemera in, you will need to determine how you want to organize the items. They can be organized by theme, style, or age. Some collectors even save their ephemera by color. It is important to choose so that you can find select pieces easier and quicker.

To mark the boxes for identification, use labels or tab dividers. You can also put an image of the outside of the box or cabinet to remember what is stored inside the box.

You can save labels in a scrapbook, notebook, or photo album. Keep a note next to each label with a message of where you picked up the label. It may be something you found or peeled from a bottle that you enjoyed personally.

Tip 94: Ways to Catalog Your Cereal Ephemera

When you organize your cereal ephemera, this can be done by manufacturers, decades, or themes. There are several themes to continue. A more creative theme is "discontinued cereals." The discontinued cereals will bring in a higher value and will make your cereal ephemera collection really pop!

- Wheat Krispies (1934)
- Corn Soya (1948)
- Corn Crackos (1967)
- Puffa Puffa Rice (1967)
- Kaboom Cereal (1969)
- Grins & Smiles & Giggles & Laughs (1975)
- Moonstones (1976)
- Crazy Cow (1976)
- Nerds Cereal (1985)
- Circus Fun (1986)
- Rocky Road Cereal (1986)
- Ice Cream Cones Cereal (1987)

Cereal can also be collected by themes such as card games, video games & board games, including Donkey Kong Crunch (1982), Pac Man (1983), Pokemon Cereal (2000), and Monopoly Cereal (2003). In addition, there are cereals with a comics theme, including Spiderman Cereal (1985), Morning Funnies (1988), and Batman Cereal (1989). There are also monster-themed cereals, Franken Berry (1971), Count Chocula (1971), Boo Berry (1973), Fruit Brute (1975), and Fruity Yummy Mummy (1987).

When Fruity Pebbles and Cocoa Pebbles were introduced in 1971, they launched a line of TV-themed cereals. Dino Pebbles debuted in 1991. Cupcake Pebbles Cereal was introduced in 2010 and only sold for a year. The movie-themed cereals followed soon after:

- Pink Panther Flakes (1972)
- Strawberry Shortcake Cereal (1982)
- E.T. Cereal (1984)
- C-3PO's Cereal (1984)

- Ghostbusters (1985)
- Rainbow Brite (1985)
- Teenage Mutant Ninja Turtles (1989)
- Bill and Ted's Excellent Cereal (1990)
- The Addam's Family (1991)
- Homer's Cinnamon Donut Cereal (1991)
- Urkel-os (1991)
- Nickelodeon Green Slime (2003)

Some cereals had a theme of their own. Cap'n Crunch cereal was introduced in 1963, and today they have the largest variety of any cereal. They could almost be an ephemera collection of their own. It all started in 1963 with regular Cap'n Crunch and grew to include Crunch Berries and Peanut Butter Crunch in 1969. After the release of Crunch Berries, it took off from there. These are just 15 of the over 100 varieties added to the Cap'n Crunch family in the years that followed:

- Oops All Berries
- Polar Crunch
- Cotton Candy Crunch
- Chocolate Caramel Crunch
- Superman Crunch
- Cinnamon Roll Crunch
- Sprinkled Donut Crunch
- Punch Crunch
- Homerun Crunch
- Cosmic Crunch
- Mystery Volcano Crunch
- Deep Sea Crunch
- Air Heads Berries
- Smashed Berries
- Orange Creampop Crunch

Tip 95: Cleaning and Repairing Ephemera Safely

Tears on paper can be fixed by using Archival Document Repair Tape. Do not use any other form of tape.

Professionals can restore fading on ephemera. They can also remove pen marks using an ink eradicator. An art gum eraser is used to remove pencil marks. Never use a regular pencil eraser. They can tear the paper and leave a smudge mark. Removing ink and pencil marks also removes the color. A professional can add the colors back to restore the look of vintage or damaged ephemera

You can dust your ephemera safely by using either a soft cloth, a paintbrush, or a toothbrush with soft bristles. A baby brush is also good for dusting ephemera. It is essential to do this before you store the ephemera. This can also be done to remove mold or mildew. When removing the mold, remember to brush it off softly in even strokes to prevent tears.

If you can do so safely, remove any sticky material, old tape, and staples. The metal from the staples can cause rust. Also, do not use cleaning material directly on ephemera. The chemicals can cause permanent damage to the paper.

Tip 96: Removing Soot and Dirt

When cleaning vintage documents, do one section at a time and lay an item on top of your vintage document to keep the paper from moving around and getting torn. The safest way to do that is to lay a sheet of paper on top of the document and put an item with weight on top of that paper – not on the vintage document that you are cleaning. For cleaning dirt from documents, use a Document Cleaning Pad. This is a rectangular-shaped cotton sponge that has a porous cover and is filled with particles of the Staedtler Mars Plastic Eraser. Shake the bag and roll it in your hands over the document to release the particles. Then use the cleaning pad to wipe the document in a circular motion.

A Dry-Cleaning Sponge also called a Soot Eraser, and a Dirt Eraser can be used to wipe across documents and photographs to clean off dirt and soot. Only wipe the sponge across in one motion, not in a back-and-forth motion. They come in large sizes and can be cut down if needed. When the top of the sponge gets black from cleaning, simply cut that part off so you can continue to use the sponge. It is important to remember not to use these erasers on documents with pencil writing. It will completely remove anything written in pencil.

Tip 97: How to Use Absorene

Absorene is a material with a texture similar to Play-Doh that can clean documents. This is particularly good with cleaning comic book covers. First, wipe the Absorene across the ephemera, swiping in one direction. This is to remove the surface dirt. After you have gone across the comic book, go over it again, this time rolling the Absorene across it. Always wipe in the direction going away from the spine. You can reuse the Absorene, but throw it away when it starts to crumble.

Tip 98: Handling Vintage Ephemera Properly

When you handle vintage ephemera, hold it on both sides. Also, wear powder-free latex gloves, vinyl, white cotton, or nylon. The gloves will protect the paper from the natural oils on your hands. The oil on your skin can damage the paper and cause it to age quicker. If you do not have gloves readily available, then wash and dry your hands before handling the ephemera. Only wash your hands with hot water. Chemicals from the soap can damage colors or vintage paper. When you handle vintage documents, hold them close to the edge. Most of the printing and images are in the center of the documents, and you want to protect that part the most.

On the back of stamps is an adhesive that can cause them to stick to your fingers or to each other. When handling them, use stamp tweezers to protect them. These tweezers are also good for handling other vintage ephemera types.

Tip 99: Safe Way to Remove Used Stamps

If there are used stamps on envelopes you want to remove for your collection; the Smithsonian National Postal Museum developed a safe and effective way to do this. These are their steps for removing stamps:

Tear or cut the envelope around the stamp.

Soak the stamp, face down, in cool water for 15-20 minutes.

When the stamp is freed from the envelope, remove it from the water using stamp tweezers.

Put the stamp between paper towels and place a heavy book on top. Keep it there for a day to dry the stamp thoroughly and straighten it; otherwise, the stamp will curl.

Tip 100: Careful Techniques for Storing Paper Money

When you are in the process of storing paper money, before you lay the bills down on any surface, make sure it is clean and dry. Do not try to clean or repair paper money. That should always be done by a professional. There are sheet protectors that are sized for paper money. Be sure the ones you use are acid-free and polyvinyl chloride (PVC) free. Look for sleeves that are made of mylar polyester material. They are designed for long-term use. You can then store the sleeves in folders or storage boxes. The paper money should fit easily with no section of the money popping out. If it is exposed, it will cause the paper money to discolor in time. Sunlight, heat, and moisture are the biggest dangers for paper money. Store the album or the box in a dresser or a cupboard where it is relatively dry, and there will not be fluctuating temperatures. Avoid areas that can be open to molds, such as the attic or basement.

Tip 101: Remember this When Storing Magazine Ephemera

Store the magazines in a cool environment with low humidity and light. Sunlight and bright lights will fade the color from the magazines. Before storing the magazines, make sure they are completely dry. Any dampness can cause mold to develop later.

When storing magazines, put a sheet of acid-free tissue paper between the pages you want to save. It can be several pages you like the most or between every page. That is up to you to decide. Then place the magazine in a plastic sleeve protector, sometimes called bags. There are three types: polyethylene, polypropylene, and polyester. Keep them in a place where they can lay flat so that it does not cause damage to the spine.

The polyethylene sleeves come in two sizes – 2 mils and 3 mils. The differences are that the 3 mils size is thicker, and the flap that closes has a resealable adhesive back. They are acid-free and water resistant. The polypropylene storage bags are 1.5 mils thick, have a resealable flap, and are also acid-free and water resistant. These covers will not yellow over time. The third style is the Polyester bags, which are 2 mils thick and made of archival armor. They are also acid-free and water resistant. These are the preferred bags used by the Library of Congress. Remember, these storage bags are not waterproof – only water resistant.

Use an archival storage box to save the magazines. Between each magazine, place a piece of acid-free backer board to keep the magazine flat. The backings also come in three styles. The first is the kcb30 backing. It is pH neutral and has a 30-point chipboard giving it a medium flexibility feel. The next is the kaf28 backing, which has a 28-point chipboard and is acid-free. The material can extend the life of your magazine. The third style is the kaf40, which has a 40-point chipboard that is acid-free, lignin-free, and alpha-cellulose fiber. In addition, it has a calcium carbonate buffer to prevent acid from forming.

Tip 102: Products Used for Storing Ephemera

Protective sheets come in a variety of sizes for storing postcards, stationery letters, and full sheets of stamps.

When you choose a plastic box or sheets for storage, select the ones that are made with Polyester (PET), Polypropylene (PP), or Polyethylene Terephthalate (PE). Avoid plastic that contains Polyvinyl Chloride (PVC). The chlorine in the plastic can bleach the paper products.

Glassine Envelopes come in different sizes. Some are small enough for one stamp and large enough for a postcard. They are resistant to air and moisture and are acid-free. You can use a marker to write on the outside to label the contents but only do this before you put the ephemera in the envelope so it does not stain the paper. You can also use a label to mark the contents. This is better protection, and they can be peeled off easily to reuse the envelopes. However, the envelopes do yellow in time. When this happens, simply switch it to a new glassine envelope.

Dealer Sales Cards are a safe way to store and organize stamps. They are made with a safe plastic cover and malignant-free cardstock. Approval cards are large enough to store several stamps and have an added cover to access the stamps easily. This helps when you want to store stamp strips or keep a series of stamps together.

Tip 103: Insuring Your Ephemera Collection

No matter how hard you work to protect your collection, life has a way of making things go terribly wrong. Floods, fires, and earthquakes are unpreventable. This is why it is important to get insurance for your collection. When choosing a plan, read the policy carefully, specifically the area that goes over what the insurance does NOT cover. Each state has a different set of regulations that they follow.

You can ensure your collection by including a rider in your homeowner's insurance policy or rental insurance. This is sometimes called an "insurance floater" or "personal property floater." Do not assume that your collection is covered. Make sure the coverage for your ephemera collection is included in the writing on your policy. There are two types of coverage. All-risk coverage protects against any incident except for the ones that they list as unaccepted. With perils coverage, they only cover items that have been damaged from one of the incidents in their list.

Pure Insurance covers a wide variety of antiques and collectibles, including ephemera. You can choose an insurance plan that gives itemized coverage or blanket coverage (which can be the better option for ephemera). For example, if your ephemera is part of a set or series and only a part of that is damaged, they can provide coverage for repairs, or you can hand over the surviving pieces and receive the value for what the set was worth.

There are several other insurance companies to choose from, including American Collectors Insurance, Antique & Collectibles Insurance Group, Progressive, State Farm, and Collectibles Insurance Services LLC. Make sure you talk to different insurance brokers before deciding on a plan so you get the cost that is affordable to you. Along with checking what is not covered in the insurance policy, ask about the deductibles, policy limits, and how the value is determined. Some require they be appraised by a professional. Another option is to determine the value through an "agreed value." This is when the collector and the insurance agent agree upon the value. Keep your own record of your collection, noting each piece, the value, and a photograph, if possible.

Tip 104: Proper Ways to Store Posters and Large Ephemera

Hanging File Charts and Poster Storage Bags can be used for storing posters, maps, blueprints, advertisements, and other large pieces of ephemera. It is best to hang these items when storing posters. Do not store them standing up because, in time, the posters will bend, causing tears or permanent creases.

The hard plastic shell can prevent them from getting bent. They are also waterproof and block out lighting that can fade the colors on the paper. You can save more than one poster in each tube.

Make sure the posters are not exposed to heat, moisture, humidity, or light. Keep them stored away from items that could fall on them. When storing them in plastic tubes, first wrap them in acid-free plastic for further protection. The plastic should be larger than the poster.

Keep a label on the outside of the tube to remember what is inside quickly. For example, you can put the name of the poster inside on the label. Another organization technique is to label them Poster A, Poster B, Poster C, etc. Then, in a separate logbook or notebook, note which posters correspond with the labels. This is helpful when you change the posters in the future. Finally, consider using the square poster storage boxes if you have several posters in your collection. They are easier to store because they can be stacked on top of each other.

Chapter 8: Buying, Selling, and Authenticating Ephemera

- Using Social Media for Buying Ephemera
- The Different Values of Ephemera
- Details of Value in the Paper Money
- Keywords that Age Ephemera
- Determining Authenticity of Posters and Autographs

Maneuvering the Process of Buying and Selling Ephemera

When the time comes to buy and sell ephemera, several key aspects must be remembered. This includes the best ways to buy and sell ephemera and how to avoid purchasing a replica. In addition, knowing how to interact with buyers and know which ones can be trusted is also important.

Tip 105: Can the Ephemera Be Used?

In most situations, collectibles are more valuable if they are new, unused, and still in the box. In the case of ephemera, gently used pieces are the ones sought after. Being used, in the case of ephemera, adds to the value. Condition is still important but being used and will only deflect from the value if the condition is extremely poor or missing pieces. That is particularly true with magazines.

Tip 106: First Steps to Buying and Selling Ephemera

When determining the value of ephemera, there are several factors to consider. Is the item rare? Can it be replaced easily? Is it original or a replica? Is it a part of a series? How has it been stored? How was it authenticated?

Once you have answered these questions, note when and where you first bought it and how much you paid for it. This will help you determine why your selling value should be. Depending where you want to sell your ephemera will determine how much you should sell it for to buyers and other dealers. The key point to remember is to know the value of your products in advance to prepare yourself for people trying to lowball the price.

When you buy ephemera, look for tears, water damage, foxing, and creases. Many collectors will even use a magnifying glass when inspecting paper.

Tip 107: Tips for Photographing Your Pieces

When you decide to sell your ephemera, you will need to take quality photographs. Before you take the photo, make sure the paper is flat and that there is nothing in the background that you do not want others to see. You can make a solid background by laying the ephemera on a pillowcase. Another suggestion is to place the ephemera on a music stand.

Make sure you have proper lighting to avoid shadows and a dark overcast. Natural light is the best to use when photographing paper. Take photographs toward the light. If the light is behind you or only overhead, then it will pick up your own shadow, specifically your hands. If you are in a low light situation, then use the camera flash.

If there are small images or words that you want the buyer to see, take several photographs that include close-ups. Have the camera set on a landscape view. If possible, use a tripod to avoid the pictures having a shaky look.

Tip 108: Best App to Photograph Ephemera

Photoscan is an app that can take full photographs without having to backup. It will also remove any glares. This will allow you to take quality photographs of ephemera while they are still inside their frames and protective sheet covers.

Tip 109: Red Flags When Buying and Trading Ephemera

When you meet fellow collectors online, whether through social media or a forum, and they want to trade ephemera pieces, there are several red flags to look out for. First, when they have little or no information about the details and value of their ephemera, they say that they will send their item once they receive your piece. They do not plan to get a tracking number when shipping out the ephemera. They will only speak privately and not in an open forum when the ephemera is graded through an unknown or foreign company. Finally, they should be willing to send photographs of what they have, including a photo of them holding the ephemera. If they will not do that, it is a red flag.

Tip 110 Benefits of Using Social Media and Apps

The largest social media site for buying and selling ephemera is eBay. They are usually the first ones collectors, and dealers go to. When buying from eBay, ask all important questions before you make the purchase. Sometimes the wording used is misleading, and when your item arrives, you are disappointed that it is not what you expected. Before you buy any ephemera, message the buyer and let them know that you are interested in the item and clarify what you believe you are buying. This is their chance to let you know if you are correct or misunderstanding the item for sale. When you collect payments, use the payment methods that the app recommends. Do not accept checks. It would be too easy for someone to "reverse the payment."

Facebook Marketplace and Mercari are popular apps for buying and selling ephemera. The Cardmarket app is specifically for all types of trading cards. OfferUp has a list of preapproved meeting places, usually near a police station or in an area with high traffic. This is an important safety factor to continue. With OfferUp, you can also sell to customers across the country.

Tip 111: Buying and Selling on Facebook

The Thrifting Lounge is a Facebook group where collectors and dealers can share resources for buying and selling. These Facebook groups can help with finding the value of your items:

- Antiques Appraisal
- eBay Thrifters
- The Thrifting Board
- Antiques Identified
- All Things Vintage and Retro
- Vintage Patterns Bazaar (pattern collectors)

The Facebook page "Buy Sell or Trade Sports Cards" is one of the largest groups on Facebook for buying and selling trading cards. Websites for buying and selling sports cards are Beckett, Kruk cards, Tonya Trade, and COMC. On Beckett, there is also a price guide to check the value of your cards. Another website to sell sports cards is Otia Sports. After your initial conversation with Otia, they will make an offer for your cards. If you accept the offer, they will also pick up the cards. Instagram is also a place for buying and selling sports cards. Follow the tags #Sportcards and #sportscardsforsale.

Tip 112: Using Forums to Buy and Sell

Forums are a prime resource for collectors and can be used to buy and sell ephemera. You can also utilize forums to research information by communicating with fellow collectors. In some cases, they can also assist in determining the value of your ephemera items.

1. Collectors Universe Forum is for buying and selling paper money.
2. Antique Lovers Forum on Facebook is for collectors of art and antiques.
3. Trading cards and Memorabilia Forum is for collectors of trading cards and autographs.
4. The Comic Book Collectors Chat Board is a forum for collectors and enthusiasts of comic books and related items.
5. Forums for autograph collectors include Autographs Forum, Markedout.com, Sportsgraphing.com, and Autograph Live!

There are several forums for sports card collectors:

- PSA Card Forums
- Sports Card Forum
- Blowout Cards Forum
- Sportscollectors.net.
- Buy, Sell & Trade – Cards & Memorabilia

Trading Cards & Memorabilia Forum

Tip 113: Websites for Ephemera Deals

The website cardcow.com is a resource for buying vintage postcards.

CineMasterpieces purchases movie posters. Collectors can reach out to them through their website, CineMasterpieces.com.

The Book and Paper Fairs website lists virtual ephemera shows and book & paper fairs across the country. They also include a video gallery from past events.

On Pat Jacobsen's website, Fruitcratelabels.com, you can buy and sell fruit crate labels. As an author of several price guides, he can also assist in determining the value of your labels.

A variety of vintage ephemera can be bought through the website Ephemera Obscura. In addition, the Ephemera Society created a list of ephemera dealers that can be found on their website, www.ephemerasociety.org/dealer-member-websites.

Antique Advertising Auctions are held several times a year at www.antiqueadvertising.com. They also have a price guide that covers over 300 types of ephemera, including catalogs, matchbooks, envelopes, insert cards, and bookmarks.

Along with buying stamps at the post office, they can also be bought and sold through stamp dealers, stamp clubs, and stamp shows. On the website stamps.org/dealers, the American Philatelic Society listed information on stamp dealers in America, Canada, Sweden, and Australia.

Tip 114: Buying and Selling Posters

One of the most respected groups to purchase movie posters is the International Vintage Poster Dealers Association. They have strict criteria that the posters must pass through before being sold to the public. Therefore, you can feel confident that these posters are authentic and valued at a fair price.

The International Vintage Poster Dealers Association was established by a group of highly respected poster dealers and collectors from around the world. They adhere to strict standards when they buy and sell posters. So if you buy a poster with the IVPDA logo, you can be confident that it is genuine.

Tip 115: Understanding the Different Values

When you buy ephemera, you will notice different terms used to describe the value of the items for sale. There are indeed different values for each item you collect; it all depends on how and why the product is being sold. These are the common terms used by collectors. You can also use these terms when valuing your own collection. When you determine the different values of your collectible pieces, note them in your record book.

Auction Value - What the price would be if it sold at an auction. This is sometimes called an "open market value."

Estate Value – The price paid for a similar item at an auction or an estate sale. This is sometimes called a "tax value."

Fair Market Value: This is a price that the buyer and seller agree upon when making a sale.

Insurance Value – The highest value given by an appraiser and an insurance agent when obtaining coverage.

Retail Value – The current selling price on the open market.

Wholesale Value -The price that a dealer pays that is typically a 50% discount.

Tip 116: Look for these Details in Paper Money

Anything above a 60 is almost new. The highest grade is 70. Paper money with a serial Number One is highly valuable. Serial numbers that are all the same or have a pattern, such as 211211211211, will also have a high value.

A web note has a higher value than a regular note. On the bottom right corner, there is a plate number. On a web note, there is just a number shown, and on a regular note, there is a letter and a number.

When they are printing paper money, if there is any error, the money is destroyed, and a new sheet is brought on to make a new set. They add a star at the end of the serial number with those bills to identify which sheet was used to print them. This is for the bookkeepers to identify for their records. This raises their value slightly, only for the significant appearance of the star.

Tip 117: How to Determine Value and Authenticity

The Heritage Collectors Society can assist in authenticating documents and autographs. They also provide appraisals and buy & sell documents and autographs.

An appraiser or an antique dealer can determine the authenticity of vintage ephemera. They do this by comparing documents and exploring the details of the paper under a microscope or infrared light. There are also chemicals that can determine if more than one type of ink was used.

Price guides and reference books can be used to determine the value of your paper pieces. They also contain information on properly storing your collection. The best price guide for stamp collectors is the Standard Postage Stamp Catalogue. Use resource books to determine if the piece is a replica.

American Society of Appraisers 800-272-8258

Appraisers Association of America 212-889-5404

International Society of Appraisers 888-472-5461

Tip 118: Key Words that Can Determine Age

Some authors coined words that we still use today. When you spot these words on your ephemera, it can help you determine the age of the item. This will protect you from sellers who age items to be older than they are. This is why with some words, it is good to know when they were initially created and, in some cases, their original meaning. These words can be found on billsides, posters, advertisements, and in books. William Shakespeare led the way for this. He is credited for creating approximately 2,000 words and phrases, including alligator, leapfrog, so-so, good riddance, eyeball, green-eyed monster, luggage, eyesore, bedazzled, naked truth, bated breath, bump, and the name "Jessica."

In 1516, Sir Thomas More crafted the word "utopia," and in 1596, Francois Rabelais gave us the word "gargantuan." Horace Walpole invented the word "serendipity" in 1754 as a way to describe happy accidents in a Persian fairy tale. Finally, Jonathan Swift created the word "yahoo" in 1725 when he wrote Gulliver's Travels. It described creatures that resembled humans.

Sir Walter Scott first used the word "freelance" in 1820 to describe a knight (soldier) who did not hold allegiance to any country in particular. The word "scientist" was coined by William Whewell in 1833. Charles Dickens invented the word "boredom" in 1853; he also coined the words cheesiness, doormat, snobbish, and rampage. Lewis Carroll coined "chortle" in 1871. Finally, mark Twain introduced the word "hard-boiled" in 1886 to describe a person who was stubborn.

There are several words that were created by authors. JM Barrie was the first to use the name "Wendy." Author, Benjamin Disraeli, started the word "millionaire" in his book, Vivian Grey. J.R.R. Tolkien created the word "tween" in 1937. Though when he wrote it, it was in reference to hobbits in their 20s. It later described children between the ages of 10 – 13. Dr. Seuss created the word "nerd" in 1950. Finally, Dr. Wayne Oates gave us the word "workaholic" in 1971.

Tip 119: Understanding Different Details in the Address

When determining the authentication and verifying the age, several details are narrowed down to the specifics in the wording. For letters, postcards, and labels that include an address, there are details in how it was written that can tell you when it was written. Changes to the format of writing an address started with the states. States were abbreviated by using the first four letters. For example, Montana would have been shortened to "Mont." Unfortunately, this caused a problem with Mississippi & Missouri, North Carolina & North Dakota, and South Carolina & South Dakota. Those state names have the same first four letters. This often caused mail to be delivered to the wrong state.

To fix the problem, the post office created a system of zip codes. They were introduced in 1963 and were mandatory. States claimed that this was confusing because it was too much to write on the last line. By October, the post office had a solution to that problem too. They established a system of two-letter abbreviations to be used for each state. By looking at how the address is written, you can get a more approximate age for vintage ephemera.

Tip 120: Magazine Grading Scale

There is a separate grading scale specifically used by collectors of magazine ephemera.

Mint (M) – The magazine looks almost brand new. There are no creases in the spine, and the cover is attached. Some may have a mailing label that will also be intact. There are no wrinkles or tears. There are no rusty staples or water stains. There are no pen marks or missing pages.

Near Mint (NM) - There can be small stress lines or light creases on the spine. Also, there can be a small chip in the corner or a tear on the bind.

Very Fine (VF) – The magazine does not lay flat. There can be some wear on the cover, on the corners, and along the edges. A few of the pages may show discoloration of yellow or tan.

Fine (F) – There can be damage to the spine and the corners. No large creases.

Very Good (VG) – The magazine shows reading wear, some discoloration, and soil marks. There can be a small chunk missing from the corner. The cover cannot show significant damage but can be a little loose. The pages can have small tears or folds.

Good (G) – The cover can be unattached. The pages must all still be there, but they can be missing pieces.

Tip 121: When Buying and Selling from Auctions

Before you participate in an auction, whether it is online or in-person, there are several things to consider. Know what you are looking for. Auctions will provide a catalog beforehand so you can choose the items that you want to purchase. By the way, those auction catalogs and bills of sales can also be added to your ephemera collection.

Do not accept the first bid. Auctioneers always start with the highest price, and the price drops. So when two people are bidding on an item that you want, wait until one of them drops out before you make your bid. That will keep the price from going too high.

Have a budget of how much you want to spend and stay with it. If you cannot stay online the whole time with the online auction, they do have the option for automatic bidding, allowing them to place your bid, keeping you the highest bidder. However, they will allow you to set a limit to how much you will allow the bidding to go. Make sure you set this to keep you within your spending limit. If this is an online auction, and you are the winning bidder, maintain contact with the seller from the day the auction ends until you receive the item(s).

The amount the seller pays when their item is sold at the auction is called the 'Seller Premium.' When an item is sold at an auction, it often includes a 'Buyer Premium.' This is a separate charge that goes to the auctioneer and is paid by the person who wins the bid.

When you sell an item at an auction, you are given the option to set a reserve. This is the minimum amount that you will accept for your item. The sale does not go through if the reserve is not met. However, you will still need to pay a fee to the auction house.

Tip 122 Know the Different Types of Auctions

You can find auction houses near you on the website auctionzip.com. There are four types of auctions. The most common is the Live Auction, which starts off with the lowest bid. In the end, the highest bidder wins.

A Dutch auction works the other way around, where the bidding starts with the highest bid, and the prices go down from there. The winner of that auction is the one that accepts the price offered.

In a Silent Auction, each person submits one bid. They do not know the bids and have to make a prediction by judging what they think others are willing to pay. The highest bidder wins that auction.

An Online Auction takes place online, and like a live auction, the highest bidder wins. These auctions often take place over a period of several days. In most cases, these auctions last 2-3 weeks. Before you start bidding, make sure you find out the shipping charges, any sizes (if it applies), and their return policy. The most common online auctions are eBay, 1st Dibs, Live Auctioneers, and Heritage Auctions.

Tip 123: Authenticating Documents with the Heritage Collectors' Society

The Heritage Collectors' Society works with autographs and historical documents that fall under these categories:

- US History
- Military & Naval
- World History
- Civil War
- 1776 American Revolution
- Declaration of Independence
- US Presidents and First Ladies
- Science & Invention
- Authors, Artists & Poets
- Sports & Entertainment
- Space Aviation & Wright Brothers

They are a prime resource for authenticating and determining the value of ephemera. They also buy, sell, and consign documents. If you are looking for specific pieces of ephemera, they can help to locate them. They have resources around the world.

Tip 124: The Importance of a Certificate of Authenticity

Obtaining a certificate of authenticity increases the value of your item because it assures the buyer that the item is not a replica but genuine. The information on a certificate of authenticity should include the name of the item, previous owner information, and any identifying numbers or details, including the production date, dimensions, and edition number. It should also include the certificate of authenticity seal. For added protection, ask to talk to the person that provided the certificate.

Tip 125: The Value of Stamps with Mistakes

Stamps that were printed with mistakes and misspellings are sought after by philatelists. In 2007, England released a series of stamps that depicted travel destinations in their country. One of them was the "Isle of Wight." However, on the stamp, it is spelled "Isle of White."

The most desirable misprinted stamp is the "Inverted Jenny." This 24-cent stamp was released in 1918. The blue and red stamp featured the Curtiss JN-4 ("Jenny") in flight. However, when it was printed, the biplane was flying upside-down. They released seven sheets of the stamp before they noticed their mistake. Each sheet contained 100 stamps. The government was able to destroy six of the sheets. The seventh sheet was sold to a stamp collector named William Robey. When Robey was informed that new stamp designs were delivered to the post office, he bought a sheet for his collection. The postal worker did not recognize the error when he handed him the stamps. Robey did spot the mistake and realized the stamp's value. He kept that information to himself and paid the $24. He later separated the stamps and sold them individually.

Tip 126: The Secret is in the Size

Movie posters were introduced in 1909 and were first known as one-sheets. You can determine an authentic movie poster from a replica based on the size. Authentic posters come in these sizes:

- Lobby Card 11" x 14"
- Window Card 14" x 22"
- Insert 14" x 36"
- Half Sheet 22" x 28"
- Three Sheet 41" x 81"
- One Sheet posters: 27" x 41" (before 1980) and 27" x 40" (after 1980)

Replica posters come in these sizes:

Lobby Card 11" x 17"

Half Sheet 20" x 30"

Insert 24" x 36"

One Sheet 26" x 39"

Tip 127: Checking Autographs for Authenticity

When collecting autographs, you will most likely find yourself with a piece that turns out to be a replica. This is because some were written by secretaries or fan club volunteers. Walt Disney was well known for doing this. In his case, it may not help to even compare autographs. To check the authenticity of your Walt Disney autograph, compare it to one that you know for certain is authentic. If you come across his signature as "Walter Disney," this is always genuine. He was known to write his first name as "Walter." It is also extremely valuable among autograph ephemera collectors.

Hold the autograph up to the light. If the autograph and paper shine through in the same light, the autograph was preprinted. The best way to check the authenticity of autographs is by comparing them to the ones you can find on eBay and Google. When doing this, turn the autographs upside-down when you compare them. This is done so that your mind is not just reading the autograph and can pick out the inconsistencies easier. As autographs age, they develop a purple-grey around the edge. With much older signatures, the edge has a brown-yellow look. This is because the iron in the ink causes the discoloration.

There are several ways to determine if an autograph was written by hand or applied with a rubber stamp. If there is a purple or silver glow around the signature, then it was added with a rubber stamp. Also, when you run your finger over the edge, you should be able to feel the texture; if you cannot feel that, then it was applied with a rubber stamp. Stamped autographs are only in black & white. If the pen color is blue, red, or purple, you can be assured that it was written by hand. If the signature was made with a felt tip pen, then it had to have been written after 1962, the year Yukio Horie invented felt tip markers and pens.

Use a magnifying glass to check for signs of hesitation between the letters. If there were none, then it was added with a rubber stamp. If there is a letter "x" or a "t" in the signature, then by using the magnifying glass, you should be able to see which line was drawn first. If there is no difference, then it was made with a rubber stamp.

Tip 128: Things to Remember when Collecting and Preserving Ephemera

The 1930s was the Golden Age of Puzzles. When the Great Depression began in 1929, carpenters and craftsmen made their own puzzles and sold them at a low price. This helped them create an income for their families. They also rented puzzles for 3-5 cents a night. Stores followed in their path and also started renting out puzzles. It is a lucky ephemera collector that can locate one of these early advertisements.

May 6 is Free Comic Book Day and is celebrated in almost every comic bookstore. Take this opportunity to add comic books to your ephemera collection.

The Facebook page SCAMMERS CALLED OUT is an excellent way to check the reputation of online sellers.

Sotheby's is known for buying and selling letters, historical documents, and manuscripts through live and online auctions.

Take the steps to preserve your ephemera. When you handle vintage paper, you are holding a piece of history in the palm of your hands.

About the Expert

Charlotte Hopkins is a freelance writer from Pennsylvania. She is an author of nine books, including her children's books, featuring Pixie Trist and Bo, and her "365 Days" series. She wrote the book, From the Dark Tunnel, about surviving child abuse, under the pen name Tori Kannyn. She was also published in Shadows & Light Anthology, Authors for Haiti, and three times in the Chicken Soup for the Soul series. She has released a line of journals and logbooks under "Kannyn Books." She is also an avid collector of several items. Her first collection was keychains. She also collects penguins, wooden boxes, miniatures (including miniature books), journals, and pens. She just started collecting Magic 8 Balls and Pen Cups. She has a fondness for writing, photography, astrology, history, museums, and everything purple!

HowExpert publishes how to guides on all topics from A to Z by everyday experts. Visit HowExpert.com to learn more.

About the Publisher

Byungjoon "BJ" Min is an author, publisher, and founder of HowExpert. He started with a dream to make money online while in college. Like most, he failed and gave up on his dream to settle for a job as a convenience store clerk. However, he hated his job so much that he decided to go for his dreams one more time, and that decision made all the difference. Eventually, he did become a fulltime internet marketer and found his niche in publishing. The mission for HowExpert is to discover, empower, and maximize everyday people's talents to ultimately make a positive impact in the world for all topics from A to Z. Visit BJMin.com and HowExpert.com to learn more. John 14:6

Recommended Resources

- HowExpert.com – How To Guides on All Topics from A to Z by Everyday Experts.
- HowExpert.com/free – Free HowExpert Email Newsletter.
- HowExpert.com/books – HowExpert Books
- HowExpert.com/courses – HowExpert Courses
- HowExpert.com/clothing – HowExpert Clothing
- HowExpert.com/membership – HowExpert Membership Site
- HowExpert.com/affiliates – HowExpert Affiliate Program
- HowExpert.com/jobs – HowExpert Jobs
- HowExpert.com/writers – Write About Your #1 Passion/Knowledge/Expertise & Become a HowExpert Author.
- HowExpert.com/resources – Additional HowExpert Recommended Resources
- YouTube.com/HowExpert – Subscribe to HowExpert YouTube.
- Instagram.com/HowExpert – Follow HowExpert on Instagram.
- Facebook.com/HowExpert – Follow HowExpert on Facebook.
- TikTok.com/@HowExpert – Follow HowExpert on TikTok.

Printed in Great Britain
by Amazon